# The 12 Rules

## of Grandparenting

A NEW LOOK
AT TRADITIONAL
ROLES AND HOW
TO BREAK THEM

Susan M. Kettmann, M.S.Ed.

Checkmark Books™

*An imprint of Facts On File, Inc.*

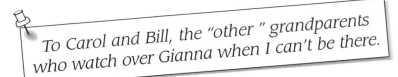

*To Carol and Bill, the "other" grandparents who watch over Gianna when I can't be there.*

THE 12 RULES OF GRANDPARENTING:
A New Look at Traditional Roles and How to Break Them

Checkmark Books
An imprint of Facts On File, Inc.
11 Penn Plaza
New York, NY 10001

**Library of Congress Cataloging-in-Publication Data**
Kettmann, Susan M.
The 12 rules of grandparenting: a new look at traditional roles and how to break them / by Susan M. Kettmann.
p.   cm.
ISBN 0-8160-3994-1 (hc)
ISBN 0-8160-3995-X (pbk)
1. Grandparenting. 2. Grandparents. I. Title.
HQ759.9.K47 1999
306.874' 5—dc21 99–31182

Checkmark Books are available at special discounts when purchased in bulk quantities for businesses, associations, institutions, or sales promotions. Please call our Special Sales Department in New York at (212) 967–8800 or (800) 322–8755.

You can find Facts On File on the World Wide Web at http://www.factsonfile.com

Text design by Evelyn Horovicz
Cover design by Maria Ilardi

Printed in the United States of America

MP FOF 10 9 8 7 6 5 4 3 2 1
   (pbk) 10 9 8 7 6 5 4 3 2 1

This book is printed on acid-free paper.

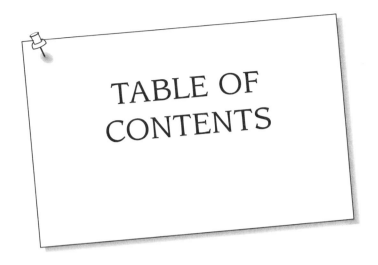

# TABLE OF CONTENTS

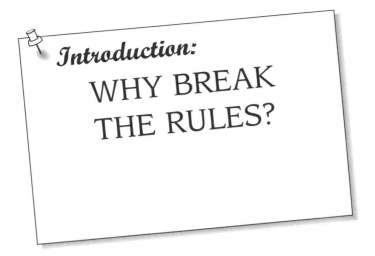

## Introduction:
# WHY BREAK
# THE RULES?

## SOME RULES ARE MADE
## TO BE BROKEN

Becoming a grandparent was a significant milestone in my life, but it wasn't one that was particularly difficult to reach. There were no credentials or lengthy application forms. There were no screenings or troublesome contracts. In fact, all I had to do was to survive my parenting years, assume a carefree empty-nest attitude, and eyeball retirement. The rest took care of itself. What could be easier?

Unfortunately, while this system keeps the human race growing, it doesn't do a great deal for people who consider grandparenting to be a serious affair. Nor is it particularly helpful to the millions of grandchildren involved.

The subject of grandparenting touches most of us. We were affected in ways great and small by our own grandparents when we were children. Then, we had children of our own and our parents and in-laws took on a whole new significance in our lives. They were no longer just Sam or Bill, Edna or Mary. They were Grandma and Grandpa.

My personal experiences as a grandchild, a parent, and a grandparent have certainly taught me to respect all that grandparenting is, but it was during my twenty years working as a child development specialist that the grandparent questions really began to flow hard and fast.

During that time, I directed and supervised a variety of school and day-care programs and was blessed with countless opportunities to observe and interact with the grandparents who appeared on our doorsteps, either as active participants or as messengers and chauffeurs. Some of them hung on the fringes, curious and shy, but content to watch what was going on. Others jumped into the middle of things, sitting on the floor and joining in the fun with gusto.

Whether they were observers or participants, it was easy to see that their role was an important one in their grandchildren's lives because the children responded so strongly to them. I also sensed differences in the ways that the children treated their grandparents, although I couldn't put my finger on the *what*s and *why*s of those differences.

While I couldn't explain what it was that I saw, the questions remained in the back of my mind throughout those twenty years. At that time there was no formal coursework in the child development field on the role of the grandparent, so I had to rely on what I saw and heard as I collected anecdotal information in an effort to satisfy my curiosity.

During this time I noticed observable changes in grandparent behavior in general. In the seventies, grandparents were the fairly predictable revered family elders. During the eighties, they began to "wobble" a bit, so to speak. They seemed less sure of themselves and there was a great deal more hand-wringing and frowning going on.

Of course there were still lots of helpful hands joining in, and the grandparents still crowed with pride over their grandchildren's accomplishments, but they seemed to have become less sure of themselves in fairly basic and pervasive ways.

In our family programs, they worried more about intruding and turned to us for more "expert" advice, even though they knew their grandchildren far more intimately than we could ever hope to. This was a fact that caused us to schedule more than a few staff meetings to dream up ways to make them feel more at ease in our programs. Nevertheless, they continued to doubt their rights to engage the staff, to give us advice (even about their own grandchildren!), or to offer suggestions. Communication became decidedly one-sided.

## Societal Changes

These were years of tremendous social change. In a review of divorce trends by the U.S. Bureau of Economic Research, it seems that national divorce rates doubled after 1965 and that the trend toward no-fault divorce had made its way into nearly every state by 1985. With divorce made easier and less socially stigmatized, the rates climbed.

The U.S. Department of Labor Women's Bureau notes that twenty years ago only three in ten families had both parents working. By comparison, in 1990, seven out of ten families had two working parents. That number is probably higher today as we move into the next decade.

Faced with rising divorce rates and parents who worked full time, grandparents were strongly affected. Their secure world and even more secure sense of role identity were pulled apart. Like everyone else, grandparents had to figure out where they fit in the new order. They had to "find" themselves.

With the nuclear family structure changing so dramatically, a great many things that were long taken for granted were suddenly up for grabs. The result was frequently bewildered children and increasingly unavailable parents and grandparents. If issues arose in our programs, we could no longer automatically assume that we should call the mother first, or even that anyone might be at home and available to take our call.

As parents struggled to make peace with challenges like divorce, the need for both parents to work, and the escalating costs of living, many grandparents stood by, wringing their hands and running in all possible directions.

For these grandparents of the eighties, it was rarely a question of a willingness to do their job, whatever that job turned out to be. They were simply bewildered by what they saw and they didn't know how to react, how to fit in meaningfully, or where to focus their efforts. They were undergoing what might be described as a kind of role confusion.

Some grandparents tried to adapt, helping their families out as best they could, trying this and that without ever being sure that they were accomplishing anything. Others were either swept away in the confusion or withdrew in anger because things hadn't turned out as they had expected.

> It was painful to learn that baking cookies and building birdhouses was no longer enough.

Where does that leave grandparents of today and tomorrow? Did the changes in family dynamics over the last few decades teach us anything about the kinds of grandparent roles that are useful today? Based on changes that followed in the nineties, the answer would be a resounding and positive "*Yes!*"

As grandparents joined into the stream of social change, a great many of them demonstrated the resilience (and nerve) to act in bold, new ways. They garnered important lessons from the breakup and redefinition of the family and carved out new ways to provide their grandchildren with their crucial intergenerational support.

Grandparents today are more fortunate. The social structure is not in a state of crisis. In large part, family changes that were so bewildering ten or even twenty years ago are now accepted as a normal part of life. We see busy dual-career families, stay-at-home mothers and/or fathers, blended families, step families, and single-parent families that, with conscious effort, thrive! These families little resemble and are no longer judged against the standards of the ways families used to be.

A lot of rule breaking has gone on and while not all of it has resulted in progress, a great deal of good has come forth.

> Fathers have become more active and supportive on the home front, and mothers have altered impossibly high standards of cooking and cleaning while working outside of the home.

## Redefined Family Roles

Mothers and fathers have redefined their roles so that their families can succeed. A good many grandparents are also finding surprisingly effective ways to support new family models. There are unlimited possibilities today for grandparents, who live both near and far from their grandchildren, to support their families in truly meaningful ways. Not so surprising, this happens best when they are willing to engage in some rule breaking of their own!

For grandparents who have leaped into the future, sorted out what to bring forward and what to leave behind, it has not been an easy task. They have given up traditional ways of doing things in favor of doing what works for them.

The traditional role of the grandparent has evolved over time and across all cultures. It is universally viewed as a sacred time of life, and it should remain so. Most cultures, notably our own, do not train grandparents for their important job. It is pretty much accepted that when the time comes, the wisdom of a lifetime will guide the way. (In other words, our parents and grandparents figured it out, and so will we!)

If you suspect that there is more to being a grandparent than slipping into an honorary title, the traditional view of being a grandparent might not be enough for you. With an open attitude and a commitment to search through your personal belief systems, you will be on your way toward understanding what it will take for *you* to become a highly effective grandparent in today's world!

Emotionally satisfying models of grandparenting have been handed down from one generation to the next, so it could be argued that they have validity. Certainly, the sanctity of grandparenting will always be a constant, and we will never want to lose connotations like love, warmth, and closeness. They are an integral part of what every grandparent needs to be.

These may be followed by others like *baby-sitting, cooking, fixing, holding,* and *giving.* Nice words, all of them. Words that you would undoubtedly love to have applied to you as a grandparent! All of these words, and the hundreds more like them, work well to describe traditional grandparents as we have come to know and love them.

Consider the word *grandparent* and note the kinds of word associations that come to mind. If you are like most people, you will think of words like *loving, cheerful, wise, available,* and *reliable.*

It would be a mistake to throw out the wisdom of many lifetimes, and that is not what is being proposed in this book. What does seem necessary today is for grandparents to question if being a traditional grandparent will be sufficient for meeting today's challenges.

More and more grandparents are learning that they can add to and enhance the traditional grandparent image and come out with something even better; grandparenting with a bright new twist!

The day-to-day realities of your grandchildren's lives little resemble those of your own children when they were youngsters. The basic realities of being a child are the same, but it is difficult today for parents, and more especially for grandparents, to carve out the quality time necessary to be effective nurturers. Because of that, grandparent actions need to be more purposeful than ever before!

This book challenges you to take an unprecedented step forward as a grandparent and to examine twelve common traditional grandparent beliefs, or rules, that have been handed down over time. They will be familiar to you and possibly even comforting. You will be able to see yourselves and your friends in them for you have undoubtedly absorbed a great deal of them into your belief system without even thinking about it.

You are invited to play with these rules to see how they feel to you as an individual and as a totally unique grandparent. It doesn't matter whether you are about to be a grandparent, or whether you have been a grandparent for years, with grandchildren who are adolescents or teenagers. The key to effective grandparenting is in learning how to act with intent and understanding. Grandchildren of any age will respond to that.

One of the most important lessons that I learned from the grandparents that I worked with over the last few decades is that those who figured out what they wanted to accomplish ahead of time were the most successful in achieving their goals. These grandparents took the time to discover and then trust in their abilities to nurture and to guide. They became the "makers" of dreams that came true. They didn't have to guess their way through ages and stages and family difficulties, hoping for the right answers to come along at the right time.

Each of the twelve rules is accompanied by basic child development information that can help you to understand what to expect from a child at any given time. By reading the rules, considering the developmental background, and trusting in your own life wisdom, you can validate exactly what it is that you want to do for your grandchildren. Then you can get busy doing it right away, whether your grandchildren are babies or teenagers.

As you design what you want to look like as a grandparent, try to resist the urge to paint yourself as the ideal, or perfect grandparent. There is no such thing. We are all human and in a weak moment, we might give too much or too little.

To make your efforts worthwhile to your grandchildren, focus on yourself with all of your wonderful quirks and peculiarities, with all of your unique talents and interests, and with all of your special hopes and dreams. Given who and what you are at this wonderful vantage point in life, you can take each rule and give it a fresh new look, as if you are seeing it for the first time.

As you do this, it will help if you make a conscious effort to disregard expectations that other people (particularly family members) have of you as a grandparent. Are you expected to be at their beck and call? Or to drop what you are doing every time they ask for your help? Are you always expected to change your plans to accommodate theirs? Remember that the only grandparent you need to make peace with is *you!*

If a rule fits comfortably, you can choose to keep it in your grandparent belief system. If it feels uncomfortable, you might want to modify it until it feels better. If it seems wrong for you no matter how you try to alter it, you might consider letting go of it, at least for the time being.

Because every grandparent–grandchild relationship is unique, the rules that are most useful to build and strengthen it will, of necessity, vary from case to case. It is even possible that the same set of grandparents can work effectively with different goals for the same grandchild.

Examining traditional grandparent rules is an exciting experience if you choose to do it, but doing it has to be a matter of conscious choice. You can go on grandparenting the way you are doing it or the way you have been taught to do it, and things will probably be fine. Or, you can shake things up and find out how powerful and fun the grandparent role can be!

As you begin, be aware that pro-cessing these ideas is not likely to happen during a television program. Nor is it necessary to review all twelve of them in depth before you can begin to make changes. Start with one or two and be fair to yourself by allowing

> When you have the courage to translate your role as a grand-parent into a personal and unique belief system, you will be more positively focused in the things that you do for your grandchildren.

sufficient time to do a good job. Extend your grandparenting journey over whatever period of time it takes to do it satisfactorily in your own mind.

Breaking the rules is more complex than it might seem at first because it involves nothing less than an evaluation of your acquired feelings, motivations, and ideals.

Delve beneath the surface of the words and try to ferret out the parts of each rule that work for you, as well as those that don't. Ask yourself how much of the rule you take for granted, and why? Try to trace back to the times and events in your life, or even in your child-hood, when you were first taught the concept.

For instance, for the first rule (Grandparents Are Cheerful) did your grandmother always smile and speak to you in a pleasant voice? Or, were you warned not to upset your grandfather with the understanding that he was fine unless you bothered him? Was a grumpy grandparent a sign that you did something wrong, or did a frown mean a comfort-ing heart-to-heart talk?

If you cannot always reach clear conclusions, don't worry. None of the grandparent beliefs that you develop as a result of reading this book are cast in concrete. You will continue to change your grandpar-ent goals even as your grandchildren grow and change.

The key is in discovering what specific things you want to do with and for your grandchildren so that you can let go of the things that are meaningless, but expected by others. When you can do this, even with one rule, you can begin to operate without guilt, obligation, or uncertainty. You might even discover that your grandchildren are more fun to be with because you, yourself, are having more fun with them!

# "HOORAY, I'M A GRANDPARENT!" (SO, WHAT DOES THAT MEAN?)

The fact that you are reading this book indicates that you are the kind of grandparent who cares. You care about guiding your grandchildren into making the right choices and you care about developing the kinds of useful belief systems that will serve them throughout their lives.

As grandparents go, you are in good company, lots and lots of good company. The U.S. Department of Labor says that you are part of a steady aging boom that is producing the fastest growing segment in our nation's population: people over the age of fifty. In fact, someone turns fifty in this country every 7.5 seconds!

*Workforce Magazine* says that America has seventy-eight million baby boomers. Presumably, most of them are grandparents, or at least granduncles or grandaunts. If we throw in grandparents in their forties and in their sixties and above, we come up with a very large group of people, indeed!

Grandparents are breaking through more than demographic patterns; they are also redefining nearly every other imaginable barrier. They hold fascinating jobs, hop across the globe, compete in marathons and triathlons, and lift weights next to youngsters half their age. (Certainly not all grandparents, but a respectable number to be sure!)

When it comes to retirement, a 1998 AARP poll notes what has become common knowledge among baby boomers; retirement does not necessarily mean idleness. Eight out of ten baby boomers say that they plan to keep working at least part time after they retire, with 17 percent of them planning to start businesses of their own.

In *The Fountain of Age,* one of the most noteworthy books on aging written in the nineties, author Betty Friedan talks about how differently aging is viewed today. She describes the lives of ordinary men and women in their fifties, sixties, and seventies who are discovering that age is an adventure, not a barrier; an adventure in careers, in intimacy, and in understanding.

As an anonymous Internet poet-grandma describes the life of the average grandparent today:

*It's Tai Chi at the mall in the mornings,*
*  and latchkey kids after school.*
*Build programs to help unwed mothers,*
*  Then help out at the day-care pool!*

Whether you are working, involved in hobbies, or spending your time at volunteer work, it is likely that you are still doing many of the same things that you did in your thirties or forties because you are taking care of yourself and you don't intend to retire to a rocking chair as you get older. Most grandparents today would find it difficult, if not impossible, to imagine themselves whittling pieces of wood or baking cakes from scratch in order to fill their time.

Many grandparents are eating smarter, exercising more, and using their leisure time in surprising new ways. Perhaps it is time for them to accept the challenge of modifying how they grandparent. Grandparenting may be a sacred task, but it is not a sacred cow!

# GETTING STARTED

One of the primary tasks of grandparents in any culture is to assist and guide the younger generation into its proper and necessary place in society. Quite simply, children must learn to survive and grandparents are one way that society passes on what has been learned, what is valuable, and what is necessary for a stable social structure.

It could be argued that traditional grandparent beliefs have operated reasonably well up until now, but when I think back on the grandparents I have known who seemed most successful, I would have to conclude that it was those who dared to run against the current from time to time.

> Grandparents help their families to understand the past so that they can adapt better to the future, and they support the sometimes painful growth that each new generation must experience as it assumes its rightful leadership role.

Your beliefs about grandparents are probably rooted in your past personal experiences. You have memories of your own grandparents, or those of your friends. Perhaps you have read books, seen movies, or heard anecdotal stories about grandparents. Your next step can be to move off from what you know about grandparenting and jump into the realm of possibilities.

Do you wish that you could have known your grandfather better? What prevented that from happening? Do you wish that your mother-in-law would visit your children empty-handed once in a while? Did you enjoy hearing the same stories over and over from a special grandparent when you were a child? You can choose to emulate or delete any of the qualities that now reside in your grandparent belief system.

This book challenges you to look at some traditional grandparent beliefs to see if modifications might enhance your understanding and enjoyment of your grandparenting role. These changes need not be earth-shattering. The ultimate goal is simply to help you define grandparenting for *you* and for *your* grandchildren!

The twelve time-honored grandparenting beliefs, or rules, presented below include things that grandparents are expected to say, to do, and to act upon in the course of carrying out their family obligations. They aren't bad rules. On the surface some of them are quite good. The question is whether they are *useful* rules for you.

The remainder of the book is a personal creative exercise in delving deeper into these twelve areas. As you examine each hallowed belief, you are encouraged to question everything that you have taken for granted about what it says. Take the concepts apart, juggle them around, add new ideas, and put them back together until they feel right for you. This process will be instantaneous for some rules, and will extend over a lengthy period of time for others. The process is not always easy, but with the grandparents I knew who did this, all felt that their efforts were well worth the results!

When you have finished, you too should have a valuable new outlook and a fresh sense of direction to guide your relationships with your grandchildren. Instead of modeling mindless, prefabricated and sometimes confining grandparent roles, you will be ready to act in ways that are focused and custom designed for and by you.

It is suggested that you read each rule section through at least once in order to get an overview of the grandparent challenges that it presents. Next, go back and explore the ideas that caught your attention, using the questions and suggestions provided at the end of each rule to delve deeper. Repeat that exercise as many times as you wish, jotting down the concrete changes that you want to try out. By dating them you will create a history of your efforts in each area so that you can further refine your plans as time goes on.

Enough about directions. It's time for you to get started on what could be the most rewarding exercise of your most rewarding life role!

## TWELVE TRADITIONAL GRANDPARENT RULES

1. Grandparents should be cheerful.
2. Grandchildren should listen to their grandparents.
3. Grandparents should love to baby-sit.
4. Grandparents should know about life.
5. Grandparents should love to spoil.
6. Grandparents should be full of fun ideas.
7. Grandparents should love all of their grandchildren the same.
8. Grandparents should love to help out.
9. Grandparents should hate to discipline.
10. Grandparents should know how to care for sick kids.
11. Bragging should be done in moderation.
12. Being a grandparent is always fun.

*Rule 1:*
# GRANDPARENTS SHOULD BE CHEERFUL

## **E**XCEPT WHEN . . .

The cheerful-grandparent rule is a good one to begin with, particularly if you are a fairly new grandparent. The image of the cheerful grandparent is likely to reside within you already. It is a part of our culture that fits in comfortably with such outdated American legacies as the stiff upper lip and Victorian responsibility.

As you begin to evaluate this rule, you will be doing nothing less than grappling with the very essence of what it means to be a grandparent. The fact that you are reading this book indicates that you have already begun this task to some degree. Now, you will get to the foundation of the whole subject.

The Hollywood image of the grandparent (*The Golden Girls, Murder She Wrote, Touched by an Angel*) is fairly stereotypical; a gently aging face set amid varying amounts of white hair. The face is calm and smiling, or at least trying to smile. It is rare to find a movie or television show that portrays a grandparent as wicked or enraged.

Of course grandparents are cheerful, and as a grandparent you should be cheerful too. Being a grandparent is cause for joy and celebration—years and years of it! The fun begins with that first marvelous fuss when you announce the impending arrival to your friends and acquaintances. Then, there is the actual joy of the birth and the unforgettable period afterward as everyone "oohs" and "aahs" at your beautiful new grandbaby. From this vantage point, being a grandparent never looked better!

1

Later (even years later) grandparents reminisce fondly about those first idyllic and highly emotional days. Truly, there is nothing quite like the excitement of having a new grandbaby in your life and it is a stage that passes far too quickly. It is a wonderful time, but when things finally settle down, the whole family (except, perhaps, for the baby) is ready for a good long nap!

The ideal of the cheerful grandparent is born in this early infancy period when there is a great deal to be cheerful about.

Post-birth excitement sets the stage for what will follow. The emotional bonding that develops during this time plays an important part in a grandparent's preparation for their role in the new grandchild's future.

At a baby's birth, grandparents are created, too. Even the noted anthropologist Margaret Mead was awestruck by the simple creation of the grandparent-grandchild relationship. In her autobiography, *Blackberry Winter,* she expresses the wonder that she felt at the birth of her own granddaughter as she says, "I suddenly realized that through no act of my own I had become biologically related to a new human being. It was the one thing that had not occurred to me before."

The grandparent bond with the new child is second only to the child's bond with the parents. The desire to see and hold the grandchild and to join in nurturing its new life is a very strong one. Additionally, but not inconsequentially, that one swift moment turns one's own child into an adult and a parent, opening up a whole myriad of new possibilities for both closeness and conflict with them. With so many things changing so quickly, it is no wonder that grandparents (both grandmothers and grandfathers) almost always feel emotionally overwhelmed!

With each new birth, grandparents are caught up in a kind of time warp. Removed, at least temporarily, from the realities of day-to-day life, today becomes both yesterday and tomorrow. This cheerful state of mind gets grandparents off to a good start, regardless of how many births they have witnessed, or how many grandchildren have come before.

No one would argue that cheerful is a good place for grandparents to begin, or that it is an excellent place to be at a good deal of the time. The question is whether it is a prudent place to be over the long haul, for even if grandparents *could* always be cheerful, would that help them

2

to accomplish worthwhile goals with their grandchildren? That question is at the center of any discussion about grandparent cheerfulness.

It is important to determine at what point, if any, a grandparent can feel justified in being out of sorts, if not downright grumpy with some part of the grandparent situation.

It turns out that being a grandparent is not a continually idyllic state, although we may be led to believe that during the first early weeks. In time, the baby has to fit into a schedule and the parents have to get back to the demands of day-to-day living.

For grandparents, the experience also begins to change. In spite of nearly overwhelming urges to do grandparently things like holding, rocking, looking, and touching, they need to step back and get out of the way. Most important, they have to take their cues from (of all things!) their own children!

From this time on, being a grandparent will mean judging if you should move forward, backward, or step aside, depending on what the situation calls for. To perform such a dance effectively, it is helpful to know yourself well so that you don't trip on your own feet!

In many cases, a grandparent's helping hands begin to get in the way for the first time. The household wants to stand on its own feet and that often means without Grandma and Grandpa lurking nearby, albeit with good intentions. As grandparents walk meekly out the door, it is not always with smiles!

It is a great shock to realize that the very children you yelled at to clean their rooms such a short time ago are now in charge of your grandchildren!

Their need for parental independence continues at some level into the immediate future, and even into the distant future if grandparents aren't willing to let go and give them some space. Grandparents can find this turnabout shocking, particularly if they have played a highly active role in caring for a newborn. It can be painful to be displaced after one has managed the household during the mother's recovery period.

When new families become more independently competent (as they are supposed to) grandparents sometimes lose their chance for their previously unlimited grandchild contact. Fortunately, that is a small price to pay for the positive growth that is taking place and it is best to let go and to resist sitting at home, fretting and dreaming up excuses to drop by and regain lost turf.

The gray-haired, smiling Hollywood grandparent is little more than a snapshot taken at a single moment in time and space and that may be why it is so difficult to emulate. Real grandparents experience the full gamut of emotions as they work to get their role right. They feel sad sometimes. There might even be a certain amount of mourning that accompanies the realization that they will never have babies of their own again. (Fortunately, the joys of the empty nest help to compensate and get us past that momentary melancholia.)

This rule challenges you to let go of feeling that you need to present a happy face whenever you are in the same room with grandchildren or their parents. Instead of trying to talk yourself into a state of continual cheerfulness, you might want to focus on your real mission; overseeing the well-being of your grandchildren, an endeavor that is quite serious.

All of the jokes about being able to visit grandchildren and leave when you get tired turn out to be true. That is the cheerful part of grandparenting. The serious part is that you can never stop making decisions about what you can, should, or should not be doing with and for your grandchildren. You are the guardian of their well-being as you watch from afar and bless them with your love and wisdom.

Clinical psychiatrist Arthur Kornhaber, founder of the Foundation for Grandparenting, warns of the difficulty of reaching the right level of grandparent involvement. On one hand, new grandparents can have a difficult time seeing their children are no longer children. They can have a hard time letting go. On the other hand, backing off too much can be taken as a sign of indifference. Grandchildren are the losers when that happens because grandparents are the safety net when parents falter.

Ultimately, efforts by new families to find workable new lifestyle patterns is weathered well by most grandparents, who discover that they still have a lot to learn about where their true value lies. Family changes demonstrate that grandparenting is *not* going to be all fun and games, primarily because someone else owns the bat and ball and they can take it home whenever they want to!

How can you begin to feel out this seemingly treacherous territory? Telling our children what to do, even when they are grown, is the most natural thing in the world for us to do. At seventy-seven, my mother still reminds me to put on a sweater when I go outside at night.

Unless a grandchild is in a dangerous situation, it is probably wise not to exercise your prerogatives to watch over and guide every time it occurs to you to do so. How many of us have witnessed a grandparent scolding their adult child for taking a new baby out too early, for allowing too many visitors, or for breast-feeding or not breast-feeding? A good rule of thumb might be to ask yourself how the advice you want to give would sound to a friend. We probably wouldn't be rude enough to tell a friend how to feed her baby or how we feel about pacifiers. The same respect should be shown with our children and their spouses.

Whatever the "problem," it is natural for grandparents to react, and to react strongly. That is what they learned to do with their children several decades ago, and it will take time to learn how to turn the tables graciously.

The ever-cheerful rule can turn ordinary grandparent challenges into guilt-inflicting inner struggles if it is followed too closely. The process of sorting out parent-grandparent viewpoints is a natural task, but it can also be a difficult one until you learn to choose your battles carefully. Cheerfulness cannot enter into the task of deciding when to intervene because this is the difficult part of grandparenting, not the fun part. Fortunately, in most cases you will be the sideline coach and not the star player.

Learning to let go of control and to become a sideline coach is easy for some grandparents and painful for others, but in the end it allows you to begin to define what you really want to accomplish as a grandparent.

New families do rely on grandparents to coach them, even if they don't say so! Parents (particularly new ones) want to be acknowledged as good parents and your approval is one way of judging if they are hitting the mark. How did it feel when a parent or in-law complimented you for the good job you were doing with your children when they were young? How much better did that feel than when you were criticized or were given disapproving looks for the toys scattered across the floor or the dishes sitting in the sink?

Parents need grandparents to acknowledge the areas at which they are competent and successful. Their job is new to them and they are learning as they are doing.

> The power of grandparent encouragement and approval is a tremendous force in helping to create healthy family dynamics!

As a grandparent, you have a great deal of expertise and a highly vested interest in your grandchildren. Most parents know and rely on that. However, by relegating yourself to the sidelines instead of to the head coaching position, you enable the parents to have faith in their own decision-making abilities. (At the same time, you can assure yourself that there are no critical mistakes taking place.)

Moving to the sidelines doesn't mean not reacting, for you are still there when something goes wrong or when your opinions are sought. The parents rely on you to react to what they are doing; to give them signals, so to speak. To do that, you need to have the ability to be cheerful, serious, concerned, resigned, curious, or any other emotion that is appropriate for the situation.

A word of preventative advice: If you want to make sure that your grandparent advice remains valid and useful, cultivate a full life of your own outside of your grandchildren and family. If you are a grandparent with a full range of interests, friends, and hobbies, you are sending the parents strong messages that they are trusted and that they can get on with their jobs while you get on with yours. The approach also allows your grandchildren to have a well-rounded grandparent as their life model, for you will be a grandparent who is interesting, active, and fun to be with!

Having a full life also means getting past the changes and sobering realities of aging without continually holding adult children or grandchildren captive audiences for complaints.

By virtue of being a grandparent, you are somewhere near the middle of your life. Evidence of that has undoubtedly come to your attention already. You will need to make continual lifestyle adjustments and modifications from this point on, but that does not mean that you cannot enjoy life as much, or even more than before! Millions of midlifers are discovering that every day. The important point to remember from a grandparent's point of view is that no one (not even *you*, yourself!) wants to hear about it on a continual basis.

It is a mistake not to let grandchildren see how you face the challenges of aging, for you are one of the very few models for the aging process that they will ever know. You can show your grandchildren that while aging is not always a cheerful experience, it can always be a positive one.

Clearly, grandparents who are interested in passing on valuable life lessons cannot pretend that life is only joyful in front of their grandchildren. Children need to see coping skills of all sorts, not just unreasonable expectations to keep smiling no matter what happens.

# WHEN DIFFICULTIES ARISE

Beyond the post-birth stage lies a great many more challenges to the cheerful-grandparent rule as parents and grandparents continue to feel their way through the unfamiliar territory of child rearing. It is rarely easy for grandparents to know when they should step in, but one thing is for certain; if cheerfulness is the standard, there will be many lost opportunities to teach children and grandchildren some of life's most important lessons.

For example, being asked to cancel an event that you have looked forward to in order to baby-sit could be accepted with a smile, or could be handled with an explanation of what your plans are and why they are important to you. Or, a grandchild who always asks what you have brought for them could be met with a new toy and a smile (in spite of your concerns about their greediness) or an offer to read any story that they would like.

Most conflicts with adult children are not important and can be brushed aside philosophically and let go. You know that the parents will make mistakes, but you also know that your grandchildren will survive them quite nicely. Your role will frequently be to get along with everyone, to be there when they need you, and to leave before they show you to the door!

As a grandparent, it is important to choose where to draw the line carefully so that you are able to smile and enjoy your role most of the time. If you work hard at cultivating a respectful attitude for the parents, it is more than likely that they will gladly come to you for advice when there are important issues and they need an outside opinion. Besides, no grandparent wants to jeopardize access to their grandchildren by getting into a fight with the parents.

Of course serious issues cannot be ignored and more will be said about them in Rule 12. For now, it is sufficient to say that grandparenting might not always be just upward slopes and elevated vistas.

If serious difficulties arise, a cheerful face will have no place at all. That is one good reason why children need both parents and grandparents. The combination of roles can provide a valuable check and balance. When a grandparent has the skills or knowledge to help out in a serious situation, there is an obligation to offer assistance in as tactful a way as possible.

Helping never means demanding, insisting, scolding, or lecturing, and the parents remain the decision makers as long as they are physically and mentally capable of doing so.

To further complicate the issue, suppose (for the sake of argument) that the adult children involved are not the easiest people to get along with. Suppose that there has never been a history of parent-child cooperation.

If grandparents have not been successful in managing the behaviors of their adult children by now, it is probably foolish to think that they can turn them into thoughtful, mature, and responsible people at this point in life.

Loving grandchildren is easy. Getting along with their parents can be the more challenging part of the package. As senior family members, grandparents can be models for how to deal effectively with life. Parents make mistakes and grandparents are there to let them do so while, at the same time, providing them with the safety net of their love and support.

Adult children deserve full attention when they need to talk and they have the right to be accepted for the way they choose to do things, as long as they aren't endangering their children. If this sounds too unpalatable, remember that accepting decisions does not necessarily mean agreeing with or approving of them. Acceptance is an acknowledgment while approval is an agreement. There is a big difference.

The bottom line is that your grandparent advice, no matter how well-intentioned, may or may not be heeded. That is something you have to learn to accept. There may be times when you feel like you are walking a frustratingly thin line as you try to be helpful, but not intrusive, but if you learn to skillfully defer to their decisions, you will accomplish far more than peacemakers who agree to anything to avoid conflict.

One of the most effective grandmothers that I ever worked with told me that when she saw her grandchild for the first time, she was speechless. She went on to say that that was an unfortunate reaction because she has been biting her tongue ever since!

# SAYING "NO!" TO STRESS

Once you acknowledge that the decision-making power rests primarily with the parents, you can begin to carve out those areas of decision making that are yours by merit of being a grandparent.

Determining your limits will be an exercise that you undertake over time as you practice your grandparenting techniques, or as new challenges emerge. However, what it is that you decide is right for you is not nearly as important as deciding that you will make necessary decisions.

> Grandparents have the right (and responsibility) to determine limits regarding any situation in which they are involved. They have the right to say what they will accept and what is comfortable or uncomfortable for them.

Some suggested grandparent rights are listed below to help you get started on defining what your ultimate role should look and feel like. While some of them may sound a little selfish on first reading, consider that their purpose is to help create comfortable relationships with the parents and grandchildren. While you might not be smiling when you claim these rights, you will be smiling inside, knowing that being honest with yourself is an important ability to demonstrate to your grandchildren.

If you haven't nurtured an open and frank relationship with the parents before, now could be the time to do so in order to improve your grandparenting satisfaction. You might find that interacting with them in this open manner is something you have wished for all along!

## A GRANDPARENT'S DECISION-MAKING RIGHTS

You have the right to put yourself first sometimes.

You have the right to feel what you feel.

You will make mistakes, but you can get past them.

You have the right to change your mind.

You can refuse unfair treatment and criticism.

You can ask for help. You don't need to go through everything alone and quietly.

You have a right to your own beliefs and convictions.

(You have acquired them over a lifetime of experience!)

Stress is another factor that can make it difficult to be cheerful. It can come from within and it can come from outside of the family unit. Sadly, there appears to be no

> Truly, grandparents get stressed like everyone else, and although they may wish to be grandparents who give and give, personal issues can limit their ability to do so.

such thing as a golden age when problems fly past your house and land on the porch next door. It is one thing to expect yourself to take the bad with the good, but when the bad comes in overly hefty doses, it is time to pull back and take a closer look at your responses to situations.

The effects of the kinds of serious family issues that are so prevalent today cannot to be taken lightly. Divorce, long hours of child care, financial pressures, and substance abuse are realities for many children, but they are also painful realities that haunt many grandparents.

And what about grandparents who finish rearing their own children only to learn that they get to do it all over again with their grandchildren? Or grandparents who become widowed, or who go through a divorce late in life and have major personal and emotional adjustments to make?

Stressed grandparents can have a difficult time meeting the needs of grandchildren. Sometimes, being around grandchildren can help grandparents to forget their troubles, but that is not always the case. Trying to hide anxiety from even very young children is almost impossible to do because young children are highly accurate interpreters of body language.

Young children become confused when the adults in their lives cannot meet their needs. They aren't able to take into consideration that a grandparent might be tired, in mourning, or worried and depressed. It could be better to admit that Grandma or Grandpa is having a difficult day and that it has nothing to do with the grandchild or their behavior.

It isn't only grandparents who get grumpy. Life can also deal children a generous dose of stress, and the effects are clearly visible on many children. A national survey taken in the late 1980s by a clinical psychologist identified a number of factors that were creating stress on American families. More than a decade later, it seems that none of them has gone away. In fact, it is probably safe to say that most of them have increased in severity. These stresses include, in rank order:

- money
- children's behavior
- lack of couple time
- unequal responsibility among family members
- poor communication with children
- not enough *me* time
- guilt for unfinished tasks
- partner relationship
- insufficient recreation time
- over-scheduled family calendars

Anything that grandparents can do to lighten the parents' load in any of these areas can contribute to happier and more stable families and marriages (and by default, to happier grandparents!). Many of the contributions that can be made in this area do not require expenditures of cash or resources, but only gifts of thoughtfulness and time.

# A POSITIVE GRANDPARENT ATTITUDE

Being a grandparent means accepting the difficulties along with the benefits. Understanding that is the first step toward cultivating the kind of positive grandparent attitude that the whole family can benefit from. A positive attitude is not the same as a cheerful one. It reflects reality rather than mere wishes.

Building a full life of your own, and outlining comfortable grandparenting boundaries can enable you to more fully enjoy the time that you spend with your grandchildren. By approaching your grandparenting role realistically, you can model attitudes that children need to see as they are growing up and learning that the world works best when it works cooperatively.

If you learn to walk silently next to the parents as they strive to adapt their viewpoints and commitments, they will be able to get to where they need to be, and you will be providing a valuable contribution to that end. Experience has taught you that life isn't a trouble-free process, but you can also be comforted in the knowledge that the pendulum swings both ways, and that difficult times are not permanent.

If you learn to work quietly and patiently, this is a truth that most parents come to recognize on their own. When parents feel secure that no one will try to take over or interfere in their roles, they become less reluctant to share decisions.

> While the parents hold the final authority over grandchildren, they still need, and will frequently welcome, your wisdom and expertise as they face the challenges of life as parents.

A superior grandparent attitude stems from having lots of reasons to get out of bed and face each new day. It comes from making sure that you are involved in things that you enjoy; perhaps a few of them even a bit outrageously! As luck would have it, grandchildren are quite good at dreaming up the outrageous!

Now, that's a challenge worth facing! More time with your precious grandchildren and more time to model the most precious gift that you can give them; healthy problem-solving habits to use throughout their lives.

Finally, a positive grandparent attitude means being able to say *No* sometimes. It means setting limits on how much and how frequently you will give of your time, talents, and money. It means ignoring ploys by the parents or grandchildren to make you feel guilty, or demands on your time that are unreasonable. It means not always changing your plans to accommodate those of other family members.

Creating boundaries that keep you feeling positive doesn't mean that you are a selfish or uncaring grandparent. Rather, it means that you are a wise grandparent who wants to be fully present when you are on duty, bringing the very best that you have to offer to your grandchildren!

## EXPLORING RULE 1 CONCEPTS

*The following questions can help you develop a more balanced grand-parenting outlook:*

### 1. Do I respect my adult children as decision makers?

*Always:*
• Great work!

*Sometimes:*
• Make a mental list of the responsibilities that you managed at their age.
• Imagine how good your mind and body would feel if you could let go of problems that are not rightfully yours anyway.
• Decide what the worst thing is that can happen and see if it is worth your intervention.

*Never:*
• A visit to a counselor could help you begin to let go of other people's concerns.
• Make a list of all of the things that your children do responsibly (get to work, do the laundry, keep food in the house, enjoy time as a family, etc.).
• Take a vacation and see if they survive without you!

### 2. Do I allow them to make mistakes, without my having to correct them?

*Always:*
• Good work!

*Sometimes:*
- Once again, think of the worst thing that can happen and decide if you can live with it.
- For the next month, make a list of the mistakes the parents make that bother you. See if there is a pattern that tells you something about them or about yourself.
- When you get angry, search your mind to see if there are other things bothering you that might be affecting your coping abilities.

*Never:*
- Develop a new hobby.
- Develop another new hobby.
- Sign up to volunteer some time with a worthy volunteer organization.

## 3. Do I respect my children as parents?

*Always:*
- And they probably respect you for that, too!

*Sometimes:*
- What do you think is their biggest problem area (money, stubbornness, laziness, etc.)? Give them a gift-wrapped book on the subject. (Suggestions can be found under Grandparent Resources in the Appendix.)
- Make a tape recording of what you wish you could say to them. Play it back to see how it sounds. (When you are finished, destroy it!)
- Write down some of the mistakes you made when you were a young parent and share it with the parents.

*Never:*
- Write down the rest of the mistakes that you made.
- Recognize that you cannot tell your grandchildren about respect if you cannot live it yourself.

## 4. Do I feel rejected as a grandparent?

*Always:*
- Search out other possible culprits. Are they especially busy right now? Has anyone been sick? Having trouble with work?
- Volunteer to help out once a week at a shelter for homeless women and children.
- Write a few sentences about the last time you had fun together with your grandchildren.

*Sometimes:*
- Give a gift certificate for lawn or cleaning services.

13

- Don't compare yourself to the other grandparents.
- Buy yourself a good novel and read it.

*Never:*
- Congratulate yourself on your even temper and mature respect for others!

## 5. Do I handle those feelings satisfactorily if they occur?

*Always:*
- Congratulate yourself on your excellent self-control.

*Sometimes:*
- Write (but do not send) grandchildren a letter outlining some of the good things that you want to teach and pass on to them.
- Take some grandchild photographs and send copies to the other grandparents.
- Discover how worthwhile *you* are to your grandchildren. The next few times that you are together, offer to do anything with them that they choose.

*Never:*
- You are missing the point! A child's ability to love knows no boundaries. There are no maximum number of recipients.
- Do not let these feelings cause you to buy grandchildren more things.
- Get to know the other grandparents better. Invite them to have lunch with you, or write to them if they live away.

## 6. Do I know when to keep quiet and when to speak up?

*Always:*
- Conflicts should be few and far between.

*Sometimes:*
- Halt caustic comments before they come out. Count to five (ten, if you are a fast counter!) before saying anything.
- When you start to say something out of line, imagine saying it to your grandchild. If that feels hurtful, don't say it.
- Imagine someone saying it to you and decide how it would feel.

*Never:*
- A counselor is in order if you have any hopes of being an effective grandparent!
- Sit, smile, and don't share *any* opinions!

## 7. Do I limit the amount of stress that I am willing to take on?

*Always:*
- Your blood pressure probably reflects this behavior!

*Sometimes:*
- Cancel at least one commitment that you have made unwillingly.
- Make a list of five things that are bothering you right now and determine if you are responsible for "accepting" them unnecessarily.
- Make a list of ten hobbies or activities that you enjoy doing. If you can't come up with ten, get started on some new ones.

*Never:*
- Ask your doctor for referrals to help you to modify your unhealthy behaviors in this area.
- Make yourself sit and read a story every time you are with grandchildren. If they live away, tape record one for them every week.
- Set aside ten minutes a day (to begin with) and do something for yourself. Take a bath, take a walk, read a magazine, etc. Log what you do for a month.

## 8. Do I model positive ways to cope with physical changes and other health issues?

*Always:*
- You are teaching your grandchildren by example.

*Sometimes:*
- Make a list of your physical complaints, throw it away when you are done.
- Offer grandchildren a healthy snack or mail one to them.
- Smile ten times the next time you are with, or talking on the telephone to grandchildren.

*Never:*
- Get used to being described as "cranky."

# GRANDCHILDREN SHOULD LISTEN TO THEIR GRANDPARENTS

## TUNING IN TO THE SAME CHANNEL

Now certainly, this should be the one rule that we can all agree on. What grandparent could possibly argue with a statement that affirms their position and validates their wisdom? Elders can save their grandchildren from making painful mistakes by pointing them out along the way, right?

In truth, few grandparents will disagree with the listen-to-us rule. Having grandchildren pay attention seems to reflect the natural order of things. The reasoning goes something like this: We've been around for quite a few years and we've faced plenty of tough challenges. Why would we want to let our grandchildren suffer through everything that we did when we could save them the trouble?

The argument can even hit raw nerves if it strays into the area of how well our children listened (or failed to listen) to our advice. And if they weren't always smart enough, perhaps our grandchildren will be.

Unfortunately, this innocent-looking rule is fraught with danger. If you don't break it, and break it completely, your desire to transmit important values and beliefs will be seriously undermined.

Grandparents who assume that they have all of the answers are also assuming that they know all of the questions!

Such one-sided reasoning can all but guarantee that meaningful dialogue and communication across the generations is inhibited.

The challenge with this rule is to determine the things that you want to pass on, and then to design effective ways to communicate them so that your grandchildren will welcome and value your advice because it is coming from you. In other words, the perceived value of your message needs to come from you and your credibility as a person, instead of on what you say.

You have had many years to accumulate wisdom and knowledge and it would be surprising if you did not have some fairly good advice to pass on. However, even if you know *exactly* what you want to pass on, it is entirely possible that it is *not* what your grandchildren will be looking for!

If you want grandchildren to accept and benefit from what you have to give, you are going to have to be more clever in your approach than simply offering them the gift of a lecture.

One enormous impediment in communication with grandchildren is what is generally termed the *generation gap*. An instructor at New York Law School sums it up as the use of life experience. Older adults have lots of it, but youth doesn't care, frequently viewing the future through the prism of their own values. As far as young people are concerned, if it doesn't concern them personally, they aren't interested in hearing about it.

Take, for instance, something as common as the use of the Internet. A survey by a national communications center found that young adults (under age eighteen) use the Internet for entertainment, socializing, and recreation. Adults from thirty-five to fifty-four years of age use it almost exclusively for business and informational purposes. Experience, or lack thereof, seems to color us differently from our grandchildren in fairly predictable ways.

To ignore the reality that you are viewing life from a different angle, can make meaningful communication all the more difficult to achieve. And if you take it as your right to have grandchildren listen to you, you are likely to end up with little more than polite smiles, affirmative head shakes, and little serious attention to your messages.

How much better to have grandchildren come to you because they have learned to respect your words from their own experience, and because they know that you are a trustworthy and fair person.

Instead of believing that your grandchildren ought to be listening to you out of respect, obligation, or courtesy, wouldn't it be better if they listened to you because you have earned that right?

By stepping back from *demanding* that they listen, and focusing on *allowing* them to listen, your chances of getting your message through can be tremendously enhanced. Your words can become like treats and rewards instead of like dreaded pronouncements.

The key to getting your grandchildren's attention is so obvious that many grandparents never think of it. To get your grandchildren to listen to you, you simply need to cultivate a purposeful habit of listening to them! Not kinda listen. Not sorta listen. And not listen when you are in the mood to do so.

Attentive listening is a learned behavior on your part, and an acquired habit on the part of your grandchildren. It takes time to cultivate this skill in grandchildren, so the earlier you begin, the more likely your success will be.

Listening means respecting a grandchild's feelings from the very beginning. Even newborns send strong messages to the adults around them. Immediately after birth, the baby will differentiate its messages by using distinctly different cries to relate different needs.

Child development specialists are busy documenting that newborns are very complex, competent little creatures. The sleepy cry, the hungry cry, and the angry cry each differ in pitch and intensity. The respectful adult naturally learns to listen and pay attention to those cues and to give the baby what it needs.

From the first time that you "meet" a new grandchild, you can begin to cultivate habits of listening and respecting. As time goes on, this will be easier and easier and your grandchild will know that you care deeply about them and that they can trust you.

As grandchildren grow, you can continue to always listen with full attention. You can listen when infants are struggling to make babbling sounds, or when toddlers are sending strong, immediate messages with single loud words. You can listen to the innumerable questions of preschoolers, and pay attention to the corny jokes that grade school grandchildren all tell.

Grandparents can listen when the conversation is a serious one and when it is light and playful. In this way, your grandchildren will learn that they can count on you to pay attention, regardless of the subject, time, or place.

It is a fast-paced world and children's messages can get lost in the shuffle of busy schedules and multiple family obligations.

If you want your grandchildren to come to you for important lessons and answers, show them from the beginning that you know how to provide quiet and calm times when they need them. Young children who look sad do not always need to be bounced in the air and teased out of their somber mood. Sometimes all they need is to be held and rocked quietly while they express what is inside.

> Rushing and hurrying aren't conducive to listening, and it is far too common for children to be answered with a distracted "uh-huh" when what they need is something far deeper and far more affirming.

There are times for raucous fun and times for quiet activities. It has been years since grandparents had to know the difference and they have their own refreshers course going on. By practicing your listening skills with each individual grandchild, you can become more familiar with each grandchild's personality and individual responses and you can get better at choosing the best strategy.

Above all, the ways in which you set the scene can mean the difference between intimacies being shared and words drifting aimlessly back and forth. Remember that complex inner thoughts and confused feelings are rarely shared during a noisy football game!

As a grandparent, you can be one of the persons in your grandchild's world who provides a forum that meets their needs for sharing what is inside of them. Knowing that they can always depend on you can make a powerful lifelong impact on them.

A strong and respectful communication relationship doesn't happen by accident and it doesn't happen suddenly. It is just one part of your overall approach to dealing with your grandchildren as individuals. Kids love to talk. Sooner or later they will reward you for your careful advances with secrets from their innermost souls, but only if you have provided them with the time and space to do so.

# FINDING WAYS TO SAY IT BETTER

When you know that you are going to be talking to grandchildren in person, some simple preparatory steps done in advance can enhance the quality and flow of your conversations. After all, you want more than exchanged pleasantries. You want information, ideas, and opinions to go back and forth. Using some of the following techniques can help you to achieve just that:

- **Give your full attention.**   Make direct eye contact that draws them to you and always screen out as many interruptions as you can. Turn on your answering machine, or take the phone off the hook. Put on soft music instead of a blaring television and keep your hands free of busy work.
- **Try not to dominate.**   At least half of any conversations with grandchildren should be spent listening. Resist feeling that because you are the adult, you should answer all of their questions or give them the answers. It might be more fun to suggest that you search for answers together so that they can experience the joy of discovery.
- **Offer subject matter but take your cues from them.**   If they chatter on about things that you aren't really interested in, get comfortable and make what they say a priority anyway.
- **Do your best to be available to talk when they want to.**   Try to be available when a grandchild wants to talk to you. If it is really impossible to converse at the time that they want, agree on a time as soon as possible when you can do it, and follow through! A grandchild reaching out, offers you precious moments that might never come at a more "convenient" time.
- **Schedule in "do-nothing" time.**   Plan in time to take a walk, bake cookies, or other low-key activities that are unhurried. When hands are busy, words flow!
- **Ask older grandchildren for their opinions.**   If you have older grandchildren, ask them their opinions on current issues like religion, politics, drugs, and violence. Listen carefully to what they have to say and question them about the consequences of what they say so that they learn to process thoughts from start to finish.
- **Ask your grandchildren to teach you something.**   Request assistance with something to make grandchildren feel useful and grown up. You've taught them plenty of things, so give them a chance to return the favor to you. Ask them to read a map for you, rearrange a cupboard, or to help you with a computer program. Thank them for their help.

For many grandparents, the main communication tool is the telephone. It is relatively cheap and a convenient way to keep in touch when distance is an issue.

Unfortunately, it isn't always easy to keep a conversation going with a grandchild that you don't know well from spending time together on a regular basis. Picking up the phone and making an impulsive call might feel great, but to get the most out of calls to grandchildren, a little preplanning usually results in higher quality conversations.

Part of the value of a phone call for the grandparent lies in just hearing the voice, but it is important to remember that it is necessary to focus on the needs and age of the grandchild who is on the other end of the line. Depending on the grandchild's age and personality, she or he might not be an avid telephone talker, or might have trouble getting into a meaningful conversation, let alone picturing the grandparent at the other end of the line.

There are a number of things that you can do ahead of time in order to enhance your time on the phone with them, including any of the following suggestions:

- **Make calls regular and predictable.** To help children become more comfortable talking with you, make your phone calls regular and expected. Setting aside a regular time to spend with each grandchild on the telephone tells them that they are special and reminds them that they are on your mind. It also enables them to organize things that they want to say, particularly in reference to past conversations.
- **Mail items that you can talk about.** To encourage better conversations with grandchildren who live far away, it can help to send a photograph of yourself to put by the telephone so they can associate it with your voice. You can also mail newspaper clippings, travel brochures, and photographs to discuss at a later date when there are lulls in the conversation. You might give them a "Telephone Folder," decorated with their name, to be kept next to the phone so everything is handy.
- **Try day-dreaming together.** If you run out of things to talk about, try day-dreaming together. Even better, make day-dreaming a regular part of your telephone conversations. Begin by saying something like, "I wish we were together today. Where could we go and what would we see?" The possibilities with such open-ended play are endless and best of all, you send a message that you care about what they are thinking!
- **Share stories about your childhood.** Your grandchildren will love it if you share stories about things that happened to you when you were their age. They will also enjoy hearing about what

21

their parents were like when they were children. You can draw closer while passing on family history.

As grandchildren grow older, the rewards of honest communication is the ultimate payoff, particularly as they approach adolescence and the teen years. Then, most families experience a certain amount of conflict provoked by the normal needs to push limits. As grandchildren enter grade school, parents recede in importance in their daily lives. By adolescence, it is possible that parents know their child less than at any other time in their upbringing.

Staying close to older grandchildren requires an extra effort because they are busy with their own friends and with their own activities. Nevertheless, if you continue to use the strong communication habits you have built into your relationships over the years, you will be poised and ready when your ear is needed.

Older grandchildren still need adult encouragement and guidance, but they are more likely to seek it from someone other than the parents. How wonderful if they can come to look to a grandparent to fill that need! Some of the following suggestions can help you to remain close even during the trying preadult periods:

- **Don't assume that you know what's going on in their lives.** Ask them, and ask specifically and often. Learn things like the names of their best friends, favorite teacher, favorite color, and most annoying pet peeve.
- **Don't just ask questions that have factual answers.** You won't learn anything new if you ask questions that can be answered with facts. Find out how they feel or think. Instead of asking who their favorite teacher is, ask what they like about their favorite teacher.
- **Encourage grandchildren to talk about the adults in their lives.** If they are angry with adults, let them know that they have the right to disagree as long as they are respectful. Sometimes, being able to express what they think is unfair is a coping strategy that makes them feel less powerless.
- **Arrange for intimate chats when you spend time together.** Take a walk or sit outside in the dark with a flashlight! See what happens!
- **Remember that teenagers are uncertain about their opinions even though they might talk a tough line.** Avoid the temptation to prove them wrong. Instead, act as a sounding board and ask questions about what they are telling you. Reassure them that you will treat what they say confidentially.

# TEACHING WITHOUT PREACHING

Developing strong communication links with grandchildren isn't the only method of transmitting important values. You can also teach by demonstrating, because actions always speak louder than words.

Consider a few of the possible grandparent roles offered below as ways to act out your convictions for the benefit of your grandchildren. The suggestions are there to get you started, and they should not limit your desires or enthusiasm. It is important to have a clear focus on which values are most important to you. Once you have decided that, the rest should flow naturally. It is difficult *not* to be convincing when you believe in something deeply.

## The Spoiler

This is often the first role that comes to mind when you think of grandparents, and most would defend it as a right they have earned. They would fight you to the end to deliver their share of treats, goodies, and attentions.

In part, they are right to see the value in giving. Receiving gifts and attentions from special people in their lives feels good and validates to children that they are important and loved.

To make sure that spoiling remains a positive act, it needs to be done with positive goals in mind. The desire to give a better gift than the other grandparent did, or to make sure that a grandchild owns the trendiest toys on the market teaches nothing.

Positive goals teach something beyond the actual gift. For example, there are gracious ways to receive and there are greedy ways. Grandparents can tutor their grandchildren in some of the differences. Likewise, well-thought-out gifts can challenge children to develop interests in science, reading, drawing, or any other suitable subject area.

Spoilers should also give with a sense of balance. Gifts are more enjoyable when they come as unexpected surprises, instead of as admission tickets to get through the front door. (Of course birthdays and holidays are exceptions.)

Gifts should be reasonable in cost, never making you wince uncomfortably at the checkout counter. If you cannot afford it, you should not be buying it. Like it or not, you teach by example and overspending is not a good lesson to impart.

Finally, no gift should be given without a gift of time accompanying it. Remember that the value is in you, not in the gift. Instead of dropping off cookies, sit down and have a tea party. Instead of leaving a new truck or doll, engage in some pretend play.

## The Historian

The role of the family historian is to repeat family stories until the next generation can tell them by themselves. As the historian, you can bring the past alive by helping grandchildren understand that they are an important part of a larger group, and that the people who came before them laughed and cried and shared the same kinds of everyday experiences that they do.

Share your own life experiences and those of their parents and other family members. Paint them pictures with words so they know what life was like before they were born.

Tell them what it was like to listen to a radio when you were a child and follow up by making your own tape recording with simple sound effects and a good story. Lay on the floor with them and share the fun listening to it together.

Admit that you told a lie when you were their age and describe what happened as a result. Share summer adventures, holiday celebrations, and beloved hobbies. Describe things that you made and see if they are interested in duplicating your efforts with you now. Tell them what your favorite book was and see if you can find a copy to share with them.

The possibilities are endless, because you have endless family stories within you. Stick with the common and the every day and they will be able to follow and identify with what you tell them.

## The Safety Net

In this role you can help to create a safe emotional place that your grandchildren can always count on. You can provide a place (in your home or over the telephone) where love is generously given and judgments are withheld.

When things go badly at home, your grandchildren can count on you to provide the kind of time-out that can help them to think things through when they are emotionally charged.

Many common parent-child conflicts can be eased just by knowing there is someone that they can let off steam with.

Perhaps your telephone can be the "hot line" where judgments are suspended and anger is released. If the parents consent, and you live nearby, your home could be designated as the getaway location when parents and children need some temporary space.

It takes time to establish this kind of supportive and safe relationship with grandchildren; a kind of relationship that is established only over time. However, once such a relationship is in place, it can remain constant throughout life, and enhance the emotional health of the entire family.

## The Hero

As a hero, you can be a powerful figure in your grandchildren's lives. By acting in bold ways, you can provide concrete examples of ways to approach life with assurance and conviction.

Don't just talk about a local decision that you disagree with. March your protest down to city hall and bring along your grandchildren with you. Let them help you to collect signatures for a worthwhile petition. Take them with you to help serve lunch at a soup kitchen.

Children learn by imitating. They will internalize the heroic behaviors that you display for them, and they will be empowered in ways that may show up years later when they become community leaders and activists.

## The Wizard

If you have an interest, you can introduce magic into your grandchildren's lives with a little flourish and a few practiced tricks. Dazzle them with a magic disappearing coin trick or a hand-is-quicker-than-the-eye card stunt. Two of Amazon's (Internet bookstore) top picks in this subject area are *101 Amazing Card Tricks* by Bob Longe and *101 Easy-To-Do-Magic Tricks* by Bill Tarr. Your local library or bookstore can suggest additional titles that are in supply.

If tricks are not your thing, there are still abundant opportunities to entertain grandchildren by showing them the extraordinary that is always within the ordinary! Things that adults take for granted are often unknown or exotic to young children. Take a quiet peek inside of an egg-filled bird nest or visit a fish hatchery during a spring run. Tour a candy factory or visit a kiln where pottery is being glazed. Whatever you choose, if it is done with a flourish and a smile, will be magic in their eyes.

## The Crony

Perhaps you wish to be seen as an exotic person in your grandchildren's eyes. Exotic need only mean out of the ordinary, so it shouldn't be hard to deliver.

What harm could come from having a picnic in the middle of the living room floor, or an ice cream sundae for breakfast? What would they think if you turned their world upside down by serving dessert first, or by putting chocolate chips into the steamed carrots? Bring out the best china, or eat with chopsticks. Sleep with your heads at the foot of the bed and wear stripes with plaids.

Acting silly from time to time can signal fun and it can also relieve the stress of a stalemated situation. Remember that as an aging person, you can get away with almost anything, while helping your grandchildren to discover the roots of their humanness. Pretend that your grandson is the king of England and that you are his servant. Lay down on the floor and use an egg timer to see who can go the longest without laughing.

You needn't be the crony all of the time, just keep them guessing so they never know when the fun will begin!

## The Mentor

As a mentor, you can influence your grandchildren's values, opinions, and ideals by exposing them to ideas that are new to them. Demonstrate your wisdom by helping them to find their own answers and by rewarding them with your pride in their success. Help them to be discoverers of the truth!

Begin when they are young by giving them lots of chances to make decisions whenever they spend time with you. Boost their confidence by letting them choose the filling for their sandwich, the bedtime story, and the pajamas they want to bring to spend the night at your home. Later, they can plan the dinner menu or select the movie for a special night out. If a neighbor or relative is ill, ask them for suggestions of ways that you might help them.

Guide decisions by offering choices when they are stuck. If breakfast is a struggle, ask them if they would like eggs or cereal. When bedtime is a problem, ask if they would like to get changed before their story or after. For homework, offer the choice of before or after dinner.

Mentoring successfully is nothing more than the accumulation of hundreds of small lessons that can give grandchildren faith in themselves to handle decisions on their own.

When grandchildren near adulthood and decisions are more important, you can rest assured that you have helped to equip them to tackle the job. And when adult advice becomes "uncool," you will still provide an acceptable alternative. (Who trusts their parents when they are adolescents?)

Your sense of security with yourself and your contentment with life, or with just one day of it, all reinforce the kinds of beliefs and values that are worth passing on!

## The Transmitter of Cultural Values

To know where you are going, you have to know where you come from. Child development experts have long recognized the importance of helping children value their roots and ethnicity in order to develop healthy self-esteem. Who can better give children information about their culture than their grandparents?

Culture includes the day-to-day parts of a child's life; the music that they hear, the food that they eat, the routines that they participate in, the celebrations that they enjoy. They are the things that make the child comfortable within their family and they are the building blocks of their future values and belief systems.

You can help your grandchildren understand what it means to belong to their particular family as no one else can. It takes no special training to do so for the knowledge of what needs to be passed on is within you and your life experiences.

Share your family's celebrations, stories, special foods, and memories by enjoying them with your grandchildren instead of just describing them. Plan ways to include grandchildren in the kinds of activities, events, and outings that you remember enjoying as a child.

To help them appreciate their family traditions even more, you can also expose them to community events, food, and music from other cultures. The messages of tolerance, appreciation, and learning will happen on their own, and you will have a lot of fun doing it together! When today's children are adults, the world will be a much smaller place and a multicultural appreciation will be necessary in order to function well in a world society.

## The Storyteller

Every family needs a storyteller to weave magic into the lives of its children. If you are willing to become a bit of a child yourself, *you* can be that storyteller.

When you were a child your mind roamed freely and you imagined a thousand stories effortlessly because you never stopped to think that it might be too hard to do. Did you ever fantasize about walking up to a bully and giving him a piece of your mind? Did you wonder what life would be like without a big sister? Perhaps you dreamed of living in Never-Never Land with Peter Pan? Grandchildren give you a chance to do it all again!

Children won't notice if you stumble and stall while you are making a story up for they aren't critics and they will love every word that comes out of your mouth. Any adult who is willing to take the time to tell them stories will be rewarded with attention, enthusiastic approval, and nagging for just one more.

When your sleepy-eyed grandchildren ask for a bedtime story, stretch their imaginations by making up a story instead of reaching for a book. It is easy to begin with stories from your own life. (You have an unlimited supply of material!) Tell them about the time you disobeyed your mother and what happened as a result. Describe what your favorite Christmas was like and why. Tell them about all the things there were to see and do on the way home from school.

When you feel comfortable, branch out into the realm of make-believe and create stories of your own. Have your grandchild suggest a beginning and take it from there. Nothing is too silly or too unreasonable to a child. If you don't know where to begin, challenge grandchildren to make up a beginning and when you get to the ending, you will know it! Storytelling is a lot like a hug. It sounds silly when you describe it, but when you do it, it feels wonderful!

## Model of Aging

The child's view of aging is not often a first-hand experience today. Senior living communities and residential-care facilities have largely replaced the care of family elders in the home. Coupled with the day-care programs that most children spend a good deal of time in, it can be difficult to provide children with day-to-day casual contact with elders and the aging process.

The need to form relationships with elders is critical to a child's understanding of the aging process and of the cycle of life. Unless children know grandparents and great-grandparents personally so that they learn to see past superficial changes, aging can be seen as a frightening, rather than a natural process.

You can model that growing old is a state of mind as well as a state of the body, by discussing aging issues in a matter-of-fact way when grandchildren ask questions (and children ask questions of the bluntest nature!). Children will accept any information given to them by an adult if it is told clearly and truthfully. By doing so to the best of your ability, you show that you respect their questions and that you are not ashamed or embarrassed by their concerns.

False teeth, wheelchairs, eyeglasses, hearing aids, and hair loss are all fair game to inquisitive youngsters. So are lifestyle modifications that keep you from running beside them, pitching a ball, or picking them up.

You can help your grandchildren experience the life cycle in its completeness as you model an acceptance of your physical changes and as you demonstrate that you enjoy life (and them!) in many ways. Having interests and hobbies and learning new things to share with them also show what the human spirit is made of.

Did you have a grandparent that you remember as crotchety and old? Grandparents who are focused on enjoying life will not be remembered that way!

## The Musician

Music is an international language. It has also been called the language of love. What better heritage could you pass on to your grandchildren than a gift like that!

One aspect of music that can be passed on is learning to perform. If you play an instrument your grandchildren will love to hear you play. Consider incorporating a few pieces into family get-togethers and encourage other performing family members to do the same.

If you have the financial resources, you might wish to help pay for music lessons or instrument rental when grandchildren reach the appropriate age and express an interest. Younger grandchildren will grow up hearing their siblings and cousins play and will look forward to the day when they are old enough to join in!

If you are not a performer, don't dismay. An appreciation for music is an equally valuable contribution to make. There are an enormous variety of live music performances to attend in any community. There are ethnic festivals at parks and farmer's markets, children's musicals and plays (especially at holidays), performances at libraries and bookstores, and at local high school and community colleges.

Exposing grandchildren to a wide variety of musical experiences in your home will also heighten their curiosity. Let them wake up to energetic African drums when they spend one night, and soft Hawaiian ballads the next time. Visit a music store and let them look and listen to their heart's content! If you are in the car, move the radio dial around and catch music sung in Spanish or Celtic.

## Exploring Rule 2 Concepts

*These questions can help you to evaluate how well you communicate with grandchildren and how you can learn to do it even better!*

### 1. Am I aware of the values that I want to pass on to my grandchildren?

*Always:*
- Congratulations! You've baked the cake and you've just added the icing!

*Sometimes:*
- Keep reading and take special note of the parts of this rule that catch your attention.
- Think of something you could do or say tomorrow to relate a chosen value to a grandchild. Ex: Honesty. Tell a story about getting too much change and wanting to keep it but returning it.

- Think about an important lesson that you learned from your mother, father, or another beloved family member. How did they teach you?

*Never:*
- Think of a personal belief that you would *never* change (hard work, telling the truth, worshiping God) and share it with your grandchild.

## 2. Can I state them clearly?

*Always:*
- Short and simple works!

*Sometimes:*
- Pare it down to two or three so you can remember them better; Ex. respect, flexibility, kindness.
- Write them down and put them on the refrigerator for a week.
- Focus on the one you would enjoy most right now.

*Never:*
- If you can't remember it, you probably can't teach it!

## 3. Am I a good listener with my grandchildren?

*Always:*
- You have learned this through careful practice (it doesn't come naturally!).
- You have discovered the joy of focusing on expressions, words, eyes, and faces.

*Sometimes:*
- When you interrupt, pinch yourself to break the habit.
- Ask your spouse or friend to remind you when you aren't listening.
- Don't answer until grandchildren signal that they are finished (raising their voice in a question, asking you a question, nodding, etc.).

*Never:*
- Pick one of the ideas above and at least get started! Habits can be changed!

## 4. Am I able to guide grandchildren into quiet conversations?

*Always:*
- You have undoubtedly done this since they were babies.

*Sometimes:*
- Go to a quiet place and let them follow you there. Tell them secrets in whispers!
- Practice following rowdy, vigorous play with a story or music to calm them down. Then begin to chat.
- Be realistic and understand that you won't always succeed!

*Never:*
• Try a copy of *What If . . .?: 450 Thought-Provoking Questions to Get Your Kids Talking, Laughing, and Thinking* by Les John Christie, or another such title at your local library or bookstore.

## 5. Am I alert to opportunities for hugs and cuddles?

*Always:*
• Your priorities are in good working order!

*Sometimes:*
• You're halfway there. Slow down and smell the roses!
• Children don't remember clean kitchens, orderly refrigerators, or neatly folded laundry. They remember hugs and kisses.
• If you missed one opportunity, create another!

*Never:*
• Impossible! No one can resist a grandchild's affection!

## 6. Do I encourage grandchildren to share their feelings?

*Always:*
• This takes real commitment!

*Sometimes:*
• Share your own feelings with a friend when you would not normally do so.
• Try asking questions that require grandchildren to share feelings. Ex: Instead of asking how school was, ask how they feel when they get a right answer? When it is recess? When a friend gets mad at them?
• Make a mistake and tell your grandchild how you feel about it. Ex: put too much water in the pancake mix.

*Never:*
• Don't waste another day missing out on all of their precious inner secrets! Share your feelings and ask about theirs.

# Rule 3:
# GRANDPARENTS SHOULD LOVE TO BABY-SIT

## EXPRESSIONS OF LOVE

Is nothing sacred? Why would it be necessary to scrutinize baby-sitting; that special time when grandparents have their grandchildren all to themselves? Baby-sitting is what grandparents love the most. It is at the top of the list, right next to goodies and treats. Why should you want to give this rule a second thought? Or, perhaps more important, are you even allowed to?

In its simplest terms, this rule says that grandparents love to take care of their grandchildren and that (by implication) they are good at it. That may be true in many cases, but when grandparents are alone and willing to be frank, many report that they are not always thrilled with the prospect and that they are afraid to say so.

Some grandparents feel that they aren't physically or mentally capable of doing it well; that it exhausts them, or makes them nervous. Others find that baby-sitting turns out to be more than they have bargained for, particularly if they have agreed to regular, or daily child care. Some are willing to do it occasionally, but have full agendas of their own and want to be sure they still have time for themselves. Finally, there are those who find that their grandchildren are difficult to control. None of these issues are easy to talk about without risking hurt feelings.

Beyond the issue of agreeing to baby-sit, there is the issue of being able to do it well and to the parents' satisfaction.

Parents might presume that the safest person their child could be with is a grandparent, but that is not always true. If love and concern were the criteria used, there would be no problem. When safety and knowledge are the yardsticks, even grandparents can be on shaky ground, particularly with very young grandchildren. It might be wise to remember that while grandparents have done it all and seen it all, there have been at least a few decades in between.

> When you baby-sit, you are borrowing your grandchildren for a designated period of time and it is presumed that when you return them, they will be in the same shape as you got them!

As you examine this rule, you will want to explore if current or future baby-sitting is being done for the right reasons, in the right ways, and in the right amounts.

For new grandchildren, you will want to give serious thought as to how long it has been since you changed a diaper, took a temperature, or coped with newborns. If it is an older grandchild, you might want to consider how to structure the task so that it is rewarding and enjoyable for both of you. The key is in being realistic with yourself and your current child-caring abilities.

When making lunch means Mary wants jelly with no peanut butter, Suzie demands peanut butter and no jelly, and Johnny ignores you completely and rolls his into a ball to dip it in his chocolate milk, you need assurance that you can handle the situation in a reasonable way.

Perhaps all that is needed is a refresher course, a good heart-to-heart talk, or even a written contract should things get out of hand. It would be a shame to opt out of baby-sitting altogether just because it is not set up with adequate forethought, for it is during times alone with grandchildren that you will grow close.

In most cases, parents and grandparents make assumptions about how the baby-sitting situation will look without actually discussing them. Both parties are limited in foreseeing the future; one for a lack of experience, and the other for outdated experience. Parents can end up feeling displaced by overbearing grandparents, and grandparents can find themselves in uncontrollable situations that they never meant to agree to.

Baby-sitting is emotionally charged from the start because it involves caring for the parents' most prized possessions. True, your grandchildren are equally precious to you, but you view them in a different context.

You know that if you make mistakes, they will survive. Parents, particularly new ones, are prone to considering every mistake to be a permanent blot on their record!

The exact issues that arise in baby-sitting will differ, depending on how the parents and grandparents view baby-sitting. As a grandparent, it is good to ask yourself how involved you want to be and to make peace with that decision, whatever it turns out to be. If you stick to what feels right, you will always do a great job.

## Those Who Do, and Those Who Don't

Consider grandparents who love to baby-sit. For these grandparents, baby-sitting is a dream come true and they will never be able to get enough of it! These grandparents sit by the phone and wait for invitations, frequently prodding the parents to get away and relax for the weekend. Baby-sitting means having the youngsters all to themselves and being able to give them their full attention, spoiling to their heart's content.

If you fall into this group, you know it. Being in this group doesn't mean that your grandchildren are more important to you, or that you love them better. It simply means that you have the emotional and physical stamina to be a surrogate parent from time to time, and that you enjoy demonstrating your love in this specific way.

You are ready to enjoy yourself in this very special way, but you might still want to thumb forward in this rule for some tips on basics that you might have forgotten.

The next grandparent group falls somewhere in the middle; not overly committed, but willing to do their fair share. Does that make them shirkers, or uncaring grandparents? Absolutely not! The emotion surrounding this rule stems from the overtones of rejection that can come when grandparents put limits on the frequency, amount, or even location of baby-sitting.

Finally, there are grandparents who hesitate when the subject comes up. These grandparents may lead busy lives of their own and feel resentment if they are asked to give up the limited time that they have to themselves. Others are too tired to perform long hours of baby-sitting after their own demanding jobs or obligations. Still yet, there are grandparents who lack the ability or patience to keep up with the demands of young children.

Whatever the reasons, these grandparents have a right and an obligation to have their reasons accepted when they communicate them to the parents.

The simplest (and most reasonable) solution is for each grandparent to work through a truthful analysis of where they stand on baby-sitting *before* it turns into an issue. If it is already a problem, it is not too late to change the situation. The level of baby-sitting, from nothing to every day, is a personal decision. It is also one that can make the single greatest positive impact on a grandparent's outlook of any rule change that they might undertake from reading this book!

If it is viewed objectively, it can provide tremendous satisfaction whether it is done once a year or every day. Only when baby-sitting is done without discussion and is not individualized to the grand-parent's personal conditions, can it create frustration.

> Baby-sitting is but one of many ways in which grandparents can be involved in their grandchildren's lives.

# READING BETWEEN THE LINES

Baby-sitting for grandchildren is an enormous responsibility, which can entail anything from a few hours during a single evening or day, to extended periods like weeks or months during vacations and school breaks. In some cases, it can mean assuming temporary custody during a family emergency.

Barring emergencies, when your assistance might be absolutely required, baby-sitting should always be by the mutual agreement of both parties. Baby-sitting is one of the best ways to get to know your grandchildren, but your grandchildren have a right to the best of you, and you can only deliver your best when your time is voluntary and you are able to give them your full love and attention.

What kinds of information do you need in order to make a fair determination of the level of involvement that is appropriate for you? Some of the main areas to be considered in this decision are outlined below.

## Ages

The ages of the grandchildren involved is a good place to begin an evaluation because of the demands that will be put on your physical abilities. (See Rule 4 for a brief developmental review of ages and stages to help you make this assessment.)

Children under the age of two require a great deal of physical attention, lifting, and chasing. Preschoolers require less direct physical demands, although their incessant chatter and movement can be equally exhausting.

It is important to remember that young children generally aren't able to focus on a single activity for more than fifteen to thirty minutes, which provides little breathing room for you. They are also largely pre-verbal, which means they will have a difficult time telling you what they want, particularly if they are tired or hungry.

As children get past the preschool age, you can relax a bit and expand your trust in their abilities to make appropriate choices on their own regarding what they would like to do with their time. Still, these children will want you to come up with new things to do to supplement what they can think of. (See Rule 6 for suggestions of fun activities that they will love!)

## Care Location

Another factor to consider is where the baby-sitting will take place. Rules for your grandchildren may differ depending on whose home is being used. The regular rules set down by the parents should always be respected, but in your own home you might want to add a few to protect your personal possessions.

If you feel the need to change rules that the grandchild is used to, that change should be discussed ahead of time with the parents. Then, the changes need to be explained as "grandparent exceptions" so that there is no confusion. For example, maybe grandchildren can taste, instead of finishing their vegetables at Grandma and Grandpa's house. Or, maybe running in the house is allowed at their home but not in yours.

There are pros and cons for each location arrangement. When considering the child's home, some of the benefits include a familiar bed for the grandchild and the knowledge that everything you could possibly need is at your fingertips. Then again, you might like the idea of not having to pick up valuable items at your home to ensure their survival, or you might have doubts about how childproof your home is.

If you prefer to provide care at your home, you can rest assured that visiting Grandma and Grandpa's home is always a special treat and that precious, lifelong memories stem from those visits. That arrangement also saves you from a drive home late at night when you are finished.

## Length of Time

The length of duty time is another important factor. Providing care for an evening is far different from providing care for a few days or for regular periods of time every day. Laundry and diapers might be fine for an evening, but might get monotonous if you are giving up your bridge group every week. Likewise, loud voices might be tolerated for an evening but not for five days in a row.

## Separation Problems

Regardless of where you decide to baby-sit and how long the stay will be, you need to be prepared for the emotional impact of problems with separation.

> Many grandparents burn themselves out by offering to do too much, only to discover that they have bitten off far more than they can handle and that it is easier to get in than to get out!

Young children generally scream and cry whenever the parents leave, even though this doesn't mean that they are rejecting the caregiver. You can be the most wonderful grandparent in the world and young grandchildren could still have trouble watching their mom and dad leave. Separation anxiety is a sign that things are on the right track, not that they are spoiled or tied too tightly to their parents. As they get older, your grandchildren will beg to stay with you and this uncomfortable stage will be little more than a memory.

## New Grandchildren

Perhaps nature has been kind enough to dim your early parenting memories. Even if you adore the thought of baby-sitting for newborns, your first step should be to understand exactly how the parents want you to do things. Baby care might come back to you like riding a bike, but you can replace a bike and not a grandchild, so it makes sense to pick up a basic parenting book (consult the suggestion under Grandparent Resources in the Appendix), or to subscribe to a family magazine with parenting articles in order to brush up.

Next, you might want to use the planning forms found later in this rule to outline your baby-sitting duty before it takes place.

# Safety

Perhaps the most critical of all areas when it comes to baby-sitting is safety. Where youngsters are concerned, safety is an adult responsibility, which means that when the parents are gone, it is yours! You may want to brush up on your first aid, or take an infant CPR class. Because an emergency hasn't happened before does not mean that one never will.

In the very least, you will want to go through the following areas to give yourself the assurance that basic safety has been checked out:

### Electrical

When people think of childproofing their homes, electrical safety is one of the most important things that comes to mind. And well it should! A 110 volt shock to a small child can be more than frightening; it can be downright dangerous! All electrical outlets within the child's reach need to be protected with good quality plastic covers that will stand up to the persistent efforts of little fingers to remove them.

### Kitchens

Playing in the kitchen is another questionable activity. Young children are especially vulnerable to burn-related injury and death. The National Safe Kids Campaign warns that children's skin is thinner than that of adults and that it burns at a lower temperature and more deeply.

Nearly 35,000 children age fourteen and under are treated for scald burns every year and 65% of these children are ages four and under. Unless children are under your direct supervision and helping you to prepare the meal, it is better if they play in an adjacent room. Even after meals, young children should not remain in a kitchen without adult supervision.

It is a good habit to cultivate using only the back burners when young grandchildren are around. If you have to use front burners, turn pot handles toward the back of the stove so that they cannot be grabbed. Hot tap water and hot foods and drinks account for the majority of scald accidents, according to the National Safe Kids Campaign, so it is important to make sure that you are aware of the location of all such items.

### Drinking water

The quality of drinking water is a concern in most communities today and you may want to consider having local water tested for lead, radon, alkalinity, dirt, and rust.

According to an Illinois coalition that has pushed for the passage of the country's largest lead abatement legislation, the Lead Elimination Action Drive notes that lead poisoning is the number one environmental threat to children's health in the United States today, and that water is as much the culprit as old, peeling paint.

There are professional water-testing services, or water-testing kits are available at hardware stores if you wish to do the testing yourself.

### Standing water

The most important rule to remember in or around water of any depth, even a few inches, is adult supervision. Children should never be left alone near even shallow standing water for a few seconds, even if they are wearing a life jacket.

Pools and hot tubs can be outfitted with battery operated alarms, which will detect disturbances to the water surface. As an extra precaution, it would pay to be nosy enough to know which neighbors have pools and hot tubs.

### Strollers

A simple outing to the mall can pose its own inherent dangers and special caution needs to be exercised in parking lots whenever you have a grandchild in a stroller. Use the parking break whenever placing a child in or taking a child out of a stroller. Most children have an irresistible urge to climb out the moment you turn around.

Another hazard not often considered is the poor visibility by other drivers of something as low as a stroller. When possible, carry the child and push the empty stroller until you are on the sidewalk.

### Car seats

How long has it been since you've seen children bouncing around unrestrained in cars? So many of these children became victims of car accidents that all fifty states eventually passed laws requiring infants and young children to ride in car seats.

Getting the right seat and having it properly installed need not be complicated. If you are providing regular transportation, it might also be easier to buy and install one in your car than to have to transfer one back and forth from the parent's car. Be sure to check weight limits and installation guidelines. Improper installation or product use could nullify protective features.

A thorough home safety check beyond these basics is in order whenever you are in charge, regardless of where you are baby-sitting. It only takes a few minutes with young children to be reminded of how active they can be and of how many things they can get into at one time!

If the care is being provided in your home, you will have no problem doing a safety check. If you are going to your grandchildren's home, it may give you more peace of mind to do a safety check there, eliminating the possibility of an accident that is not your fault but which could happen while you are in charge. This will also help to familiarize you with the location of everything in the home.

This checklist can help you to get started with reaching that peace of mind.

**CHILD SAFETY CHECKLIST**

*Indoors*

chemicals, cleaners locked

electric outlets covered

small articles and objects out of reach

colognes, aftershaves, perfumes, nail
    polish removers out of reach

no long tablecloths

loops cut on all mini/venetian blind cords

no plastic bags

location of all scissors and knives checked

matches stored in tight container

ashtrays out of reach

window screens cannot be pushed out

cribs away from radiators or heaters

cribs slats no more than 2 3/8 inches
    apart; mattress fits snugly

living plants out of reach

*Outdoors*

pools fenced off; hot tubs covered

lawn mushrooms removed

yard and garage checked for black widows

garden tools stored

In the event of a natural emergency, remaining calm is essential to making good decisions and to keeping your grandchildren from becoming fearful. The best way to enhance your readiness for such an event is to have the things you would need on hand before an emergency ever happens. That means checking supplies at your home, at your grandchildren's homes, and in your car in the event that you are traveling at the time. Your local Red Cross can give you a list of exactly what you should have on hand.

Grandchildren can and do get hurt on a rather regular basis, so why not put together a simple first-aid kit with the items listed below to keep *with you* wherever your grandchildren are in your care?

**BABY-SITTING SAFETY KIT**

plastic zipper pouch to hold:
small first-aid book
basic first-aid items
telephone numbers of physicians, parents,
   poison control center
vital medical information (allergies,
   special medications, etc.)
medical release form

**SAMPLE MEDICAL RELEASE FORM**

Child's name
Address
Birth date
Medical insurance carrier and policy number
Allergies
"I hereby give consent to _____ to administer or call for
   emergency care for my child. If it is not possible to locate
   me, any expenses incurred will be paid for by me."
Signature
Date

# NEGOTIATING YOUR "CONTRACT"

While a formal written contract to care for grandchildren isn't necessary, it is something that is wise to do in concept.

If you are currently baby-sitting and there are areas of the job that need changing, now could be the perfect time to negotiate a fresh start. If you aren't sure how to broach the subject, you can tell the parents that you read a good article about baby-sitting and that you would love to go over some areas that you have never talked about before.

If you are going to begin to baby-sit a new grandchild, a pre-discussion is critical to getting things off to a good start. You can be thankful that you are able to do this before expectations are set into place. The task will require setting aside an adequate amount of time to discuss the vital issues involved. If your baby-sitting will be on a regular basis, a great deal of structure is advisable.

According to the National Center for Educational Statistics, some twenty million preschoolers and school-age children are dropped off at some kind of child care while their parents go to work. About 17% of these children are cared for by grandparents.

> A loosely conceived plan that relies only on good will and the fact that everyone is related can be a disaster! Plenty of time needs to be set aside to discuss the issues that will arise before they actually happen and before emotions are involved in the reactions.

Grandparents are highly important resources in the endeavor to assure that the children of working parents are well cared for. When grandparents willingly assume the role of a full-time caregiver, children and their families benefit and the whole network of the community is strengthened.

Willing grandparents love and supervise the growth and development of their grandchildren as only a family member can. Such care is shared parenting in the finest sense for it is done out of love, rather than for financial benefit.

The ERIC Clearinghouse on Elementary and Early Childhood Education notes that half of all mothers with children under one year of age are now working outside of their homes. Grandparents who live near their newborn grandchildren can be an excellent source of assistance for at least the first few critical months in these babies' lives.

The need for grandparent assistance is further heightened by the fact that infant care is in short supply in nearly every community in the country, with quality infant care being a commodity that is inconsistent. The National Association for the Education of Young Children (NAEYC) notes in a 1997 statement entitled "Early Years Are Learning Years" that as many as 40% of infant and toddler care settings may be potentially harmful to children's healthy development.

If there is a good match between the outlook and philosophy of the parents and grandparents, things are likely to work well. If there are areas where agreement cannot be reached, the grandparent is the one who needs to defer. For daily child care to work grandparents should always feel comfortable sharing their views, but it is wrong for them to expect to have the final say just because of the number of hours that they are putting into the job.

At a minimum, the following areas should be discussed completely and honestly until everyone is satisfied with the outcomes, or is at least able to agree to a compromise.

## Housework

One issue that rarely comes up, but frequently becomes an issue later, is housework and cleaning. If you are a grandparent who loves to baby-sit, housework while you are caregiving might not even cross your mind. Grandparents who baby-sit out of a sense of obligation can have a harder time fighting off the urge to dig in and clean house while they are there.

The safest approach is to keep the two tasks separate and to always ask before lending too much of a helping hand. If the parents say, "hands off" (even if it is a messy house), it is their right to do so and you would be wise to bring along a good book or turn on the television, keeping your hands to yourself.

Ditto with scanning the kitchen and deciding that the dish towels would really work better next to the sink, or that the cups should be closer to the dishwasher. Rearranging belongings is a highly personal intrusion, as is sorting the laundry or cleaning out the refrigerator.

If you feel the urge to do such things, sit down on the floor and play with the grandkids because in ten or fifteen years they won't remember that you did the dishes with an expert hand, or that you could wash a floor like the best of them. What they might remember is that you were a master at putting puzzles together, or at rolling around and giggling!

## Jealous Feelings

In spite of their best intentions, parents can (and do!) get jealous of the attachment that their children form to their baby-sitters, even if that person is a grandparent.

Parents who confided this experience of jealousy to me over the years also readily admitted that the root of the problem was their sense of sadness and guilt at having to share childhood firsts through some-one else's eyes. This does not diminish because that someone is a family member such as a grandparent.

If you are a grandparent caregiver you might be perfectly free of any bad intent, but your excitement over the wonderful experiences that you have each day can be perceived as gloating over the fact that you were there when the parent wasn't.

Missing special moments is a reality that working parents have to deal with, but it is a difficult reality and one that grandparents need to be vigilant about. To help you keep the right perspective if you are in this position, you might consider a few of these thoughts to enhance your sensitivity in this area:

The child isn't yours, you are just a helper.

Your views might be different, but you need to do it their way.

Your grandchildren will act differently with you, so avoid saying things like, "She never does that with me!"

Blaming, preaching, and warning have no place in a baby-sitting agreement.

Don't put the parents down for doing things differently than you would.

Don't gloat over the wonderful things you get to see and do while they are gone.

Remember that the beginning and end of each day are the most difficult times of the day for children and parents.

Admit when you are wrong, and apologize.

## Eating

Getting food into a child can take on incredible, out of proportion signifi-cance to baby-sitters, and that can be even more true when that person is a grandparent. Fueling the body and gaining weight are not the only purposes that meals are served to your children. Meals also provide valuable chances to interact and exchange pleasantries and conversations.

Meals should be approached in a leisurely manner, not absentmindedly or as a necessary chore. It should not have to be your responsibility to make up menus or introduce new foods if the child is a fussy eater. It will be helpful to jot down the amounts and kinds of foods your grandchildren eat while you are in charge so the parents can plan for later meals after you leave.

When it comes to the logistics of mealtimes, it is important to understand the parents' wishes on the following food-related questions ahead of time:

---

*For babies*

How will feedings be handled (how often, how much, etc.)?
When will weaning take place and will you be involved?
Will there be a scheduled or demand feeding?
Who will add new foods?

*For older children*

Are there limits to the amount of food the parents want
    the children to consume?
What if a child refuses to eat?
What if a child becomes hungry between meals?
Can you provide your own treats?
If a child is a fussy eater, how do each of you view this?

---

## Diapering

A young infant can get an ugly diaper rash in a matter of hours and you could be the one left shouldering the blame. One way to safeguard yourself on this sensitive issue is to jot down notes describing all diaper changes and bowel movements so that problems can be spotted before they get out of hand.

Find out what medications or ointments the parents want you to use to treat any rashes and follow their procedures exactly, or call them for new directions if anything unusual happens. Talking about the following diapering questions ahead of time can assist you in performing wisely in this area:

What kind of diapers will be used and
    what should you do with soiled ones?
How often should you change diapers?
How should diaper rash be treated?
When should the parents be called?

## Toddlers and Toileting

With toddler grandchildren there can be issues with toilet training. Trends on how and when training should be accomplished change with the times. Let the parents make these decisions and do it their way. Make it clear that you will never force a toddler grandchild to sit on a toilet. After all, you know that all children get trained eventually and that next month is as good as this month. Get specific parental guidance on the following:

When will toilet training begin?
How (specifically) will it be done?
How should toileting accidents be handled?
Will a reward system be used?

## Discipline

Even grandparents who love to baby-sit squirm at the thought of scolding and punishing, but if you are watching your grandchildren for even a few hours every day, you will need to help out with the process of teaching them which behaviors are acceptable and which are not. This is not the fun part of baby-sitting but you can be assured that it will not get in the way of a loving relationship if it is done consistently and calmly.

No discipline is appropriate for children under age two as they are not yet able to understand the cause and effect involved. It is generally easiest to pick up the out-of-sorts youngster and to distract or move him or her. Older children need more consistent and clear guidance.

If you can't remember the kinds of behaviors that can be reasonably expected from a child of any particular age, pick up a good parenting book and review it so that you can have realistic expectations. Two useful selections are *Beyond Discipline* by Edward Christophersen and *Boundaries with Kids* by Henry Cloud and John Townsend. Librarians and bookstore personnel can suggest other titles.

Make sure to discuss the following discipline areas with sitters so that grandchildren don't get mixed messages from the change of caregivers, and so that you feel absolutely comfortable with your role:

Which behaviors bother the parents?

Which bother you?

What will the consequences be if the child displays unacceptable behaviors?

How will positive behaviors be reinforced?

What limits do the parents want to set?

Are there any rules that you would like added for your own comfort?

Do you feel that the parents are too strict, or too lenient?

Might you be either of those?


## Communication

The key to making a baby-sitting arrangement enjoyable and rewarding for the parents and grandparents is good communications. That can be best achieved by giving the parents as accurate a picture of your time with grandchildren as possible. Misunderstandings can also be minimized if you are able to talk with parents either at the beginning or end of the day, or by phone later each night.

It is helpful if you create a written record of how the day went, detailing feedings, toileting, and other facts that parents will need to plan the end of the day. If it is permissible to call them during the day, you might do so in order to share anecdotal material about how things are going, or to enhance their peace of mind.

The following areas will also be beneficial to review together when planning good communication links:

How and when can the parents be called during the day?
When will daily discussions be held?
How can you find out how last night and this morning went?
How will new issues be addressed?

## Backup Plans

There will be times when you are either ill or have another appointment to keep during the hours you are supposed to provide child care. It would be unrealistic to expect that you will always be able to hold up your end of the child-care bargain. If you are ill, it can be impossible to cope adequately with children's demands.

Sit down with the parents and make up a list of backup care, which could include other relatives, friends, or neighbors. Review the following questions in your planning:

If you are ill or need a day off, what will the plan of action be?
Will you care for a child that is ill?
Is it medically safe for you to do so?

## Assuring for Your Needs

Finally, it is important that your own thoughts and needs be fully expressed beforehand so that you can avoid situations that are uncomfortable to you. You will want to be especially careful about promising all of your free time, or of giving up too many of your hobbies and outside interests. It is your responsibility to guard your own health as carefully as your grandchildren's and to cut back at the first sign of stress or fatigue.

# WHEN YOU WOULD RATHER SAY "NO, THANK YOU!"

Agreeing to provide daily care is not a simple decision. Grandparents who do it out of a sense of guilt, or from fear of hurt feelings, can come to resent the changes in their lifestyles that result.

One good approach to declining is to offer constructive help with locating other child-care options. Grandparents can assist with the child-care search, which for infants can take months of telephone screening just to glean a few likely prospects. By offering to help with prescreening and initial visits, grandparents can

> The decision to baby-sit has nothing to do with how much grandparents love their grandchildren and if they don't want to baby-sit every day, they are well within their rights to say so.

provide the parents with a list of promising leads. And who can better identify a loving and stable situation for a child than a grandparent?

Grandparents can volunteer to handle the inevitable days when either the caregiver or grandchildren are ill. It is also valuable if they can be available for midday emergency pickups, no small contribution to working parents.

The available outside child-care choices that you might find yourself investigating are much the same as when you were a parent, except they are more fully developed and systematized now because so many parents are working. Understanding the terms used in searching for child care can help you to communicate more productively.

## In-Home Child Care

In this choice a sitter, nanny, or *au pair* comes into the home to provide the care. This arrangement minimizes disturbances in schedules and keeps children in familiar surroundings. The parents can often negotiate for light housekeeping, cooking, and laundry services along with the child care.

On the downside, this system of care is not monitored by any governmental agency and reference checks that the family makes are the only safeguards. If a broker or agency is used, referrals and any prior business complaints still need to be checked thoroughly. The child is alone with one person so that illness and vacations can be difficult for parents and there are usually no playmates.

## Family Home Child Care

The National Center for Educational Statistics says that nearly half of all children in America who use child care can be found in a family home child-care setting either with a family member or nonfamily member.

The care is provided in the home of the caregiver, who normally has a small group of children to care for. This choice provides for a strong possibility for individual attention because of the group size (generally four to eight with one caregiver). Food is frequently home cooked, and the nap area is usually removed from the play area.

There are the advantages of playmates and the homelike environment, which makes many parents more comfortable. In most states, licensing or registration is required. You can check your state's requirements by contacting a state social service office.

Negative aspects of in-home care include the chance of the caregiver's illness or vacation, and the uncertainty of having the child alone with one person.

## Child-Care Centers

A child-care center is an institution that provides for the care of a larger number of children, generally somewhere between twenty to two hundred. The care often includes an educational component and there is the social benefit of having playmates of a similar age.

Staff at these centers have educational or experience requirements in most states, and the site may be monitored for safety and health standards by local governmental agencies. Potential drawbacks include larger and noisier group sizes and less chance for individual attention.

## EXPLORING RULE 3 CONCEPTS

*Explore these issues to see if you are comfortable with your current baby-sitting status.*

### 1. Am I physically and emotionally able to baby-sit?

*Always:*
- If this is your dream and their's, jump in!

*Sometimes:*
- If you have doubts, test them out carefully until you are clear on your limits.
- Tell the parents about your concerns and offer to baby-sit in a limited fashion, or to help out in other ways (shopping, errands, cooking, etc.).

- Enjoy visits and family get-togethers when you are not the primary caregiver.

*Never:*
- Get on with other options to show your love.

## 2. Do I agree to baby-sit when I don't really want to?

*Always:*
Your grandchildren deserve better than this.

*Sometimes:*
- Next time call back and cancel with a full explanation.
- Negotiate a shorter time if you feel you can do a limited stint.
- Make a list of what you think will happen if you say no.

*Never:*
- Good for you! When you do baby-sit you undoubtedly enjoy it and do it well.

## 3. Do I feel comfortable bringing up any issue that arises?

*Always:*
- You are nurturing healthy family relationships.

*Sometimes:*
- If it depends on your mood, work on recognizing that.
- Give the gift of a book on the difficult subject area. The next time you are alone, ask them how they liked the book. (Suggestions can be found under Grandparent Resources in the Appendix.)
- Consider if you are more afraid of being embarrassed, or of their being hurt or angry. Share this rule section with them.

*Never:*
- Baby-sitting should be eliminated as an option.

## 4. Do I enjoy baby-sitting for grandchildren of all ages?

*Always:*
- You are a parent's dream!

*Sometimes:*
- Identify uncomfortable situations (difficult bedtimes, fussy eaters) and talk to the parents about limits that could help to remedy them.
- During those stages, interact in ways other than baby-sitting (telephoning, writing, visiting).

- Some stages are more fun than others. That doesn't mean that you love a grandchild less during them.

*Never:*
- Enjoy the stages that work and admit to those that don't. See "Sometimes" bullet #2, above.

## 5. Can I control grandchildren's behavior without becoming overly frustrated?

*Always:*
- You've done your homework somewhere along the line.

*Sometimes:*
- When you feel anxious, write down the cause in order to identify why (time of the day, child's personality, length of baby-sitting, tired child or grandparent).
- Give more grandchildren more physical affection, compliments on good behavior, and focused attention.
- Admit that you are human and tell grandchildren how you feel.

*Never:*
- Invest in a good book on discipline and refer back to the section in this rule discussing discipline.

## 6. Can I visit grandchildren without having to clean and change things around.

*Always:*
- Lucky grandchildren! They have you all to themselves!

*Sometimes:*
- Consider what the mess you want to clean up now will look like after you leave.
- Ask your spouse or a friend to switch two cupboards or drawers in your house without telling you ahead of time.
- Clean up your grandchild's room and watch everything revert within ten minutes.

*Never:*
- Tie a string around each finger and try to explain why they are there to grandchildren.

## 7. Can I accept doing things the parents' way?

*Always:*
- Can you really be human?

*Sometimes:*
- Congratulate yourself on things you do their way.
- Spend the rest of your time working on those that you don't.
- Do a reality check to see if conflicts are within the issue or within your relationship with the parents.

*Never:*
- It is possible that they don't even want you to baby-sit!

## Rule 4:
# GRANDPARENTS SHOULD KNOW ABOUT LIFE

## HAZY (AND SELECTIVE) MEMORIES

The pride that comes from gaining wisdom over the years is a positive part of growing older. From your present vantage point, you can look back on difficult times and understand how you dealt with them more clearly. The same is likely to be true when you look back on your experiences as a parent.

> As a parent things might not have gone quite like you expected, but for the most part you did your best and things turned out fine.

Many a senior bridge or golf game is sprinkled with recollections of parenting days: running until you were blue in the face behind a two-wheel bike, calling a child to task for telling a lie, or agonizing (along with your child) through each line of a school play. Having been a parent, you can take pride in knowing that you have experienced and accomplished a great deal!

The question with this rule is not whether you have learned anything, but whether what you have learned is useful today for today's children. The answer will rarely be simple because it will depend on how well you can assess what has changed and what has remained the same.

There are some basic developmental principles that can always be counted on. Most babies crawl before they walk, four-year-olds almost always love to talk, and seven-year-olds enjoy experimenting with writing and reading. What is up for grabs are ways to manage the turn-of-the-century family and rapidly changing technology.

It is important to accept that your grandchildren operate in settings that may not be familiar to you. You might know your way around a baseball diamond, but how comfortable are you with a CD-ROM or a video game? Although a great deal of your accumulated wisdom will apply, there is a distinct possibility that unknown factors will also be at work.

The danger in buying into this rule lock, stock, and barrel is that if you insist that what you know from your past is all that you need in order to be an effective grandparent, you could miss out completely on new information that can help you understand your grandchildren today.

Think back to your own childhood and it won't take long to see that while your grandchildren play with some pretty amazing technology, they rarely, if ever, experience such creative joys of listening to a radio, building a tree house, or buying a soda at a corner market where the owner knows your name.

Children haven't changed, but their ways of interacting with the world around them has. Their world is a bullet-fast, hyper-loaded experience and anything that moves too slowly can quickly cause boredom.

You will always have more than enough opportunities to teach your grandchildren values that are important to you, but in order to do that, two things are required. First, you will need the ability to be flexible with change and to give even the youngest of grandchildren the chance to teach you what they know. Second, you need a realistic understanding of how a grandchild of any particular age can be expected to behave and what they are capable of learning and doing.

If you can combine an open attitude with developmental understanding, you can implant any thought, ideal, or value without ever preaching a word. You might never win at a video game match, but you can certainly show that you are willing to learn as you teach them about sportsmanship, self-control, and the value of friendship.

Reading through the following developmental information can help to refresh your memory of things that were once so familiar to you. Then you will be ready to play and teach at the same time.

# RECALLING AGES AND STAGES

## Infants

Research is giving us a great deal of information about what newborns and babies can do and some of the findings are nothing short of phenomenal! Our own parents were told that we were helpless little blobs that could not see, hear, or think. Even the most progressive Yale scientist of the fifties, Dr. Arnold Gesell, wrote in his classic parenting book, *The First Five Years,* that the human infant ". . . is not fully born until he is about four weeks of age."

Today we know better. Dr. Lewis of the Robert Wood Johnson Medical School says, "We used to think that we should give infants plenty of rest and peace and quiet. But now we know that a baby can profit from early stimulation and activity. The human baby is designed to interact with and learn from the environment."

Research emphasizes that newborns are competent and complex little creatures. Cornell University studies have shown that at birth, babies can distinguish patterns, movement, light, dark, and colors. They have a finely discriminating sense of smell, functioning tastebuds, alert learning capacities, and even a sweet tooth! These capacities don't develop at the moment of birth, but are in use even before they make their grand entrances into the world!

One of the first tasks that babies face is to organize their waking and sleeping patterns to fit in with the rest of the family. (Parents struggle right along with them, learning how to assist them with the transitions.) Babies come into and out of different states of consciousness each day, ranging from deep sleep to uncontrolled and wide-awake crying. All of this learning and getting acquainted makes this a challenging time!

Babies love to hear people talk and they learn quickly to recognize the familiar voices of family members. They can't speak yet, but they love the human voice and understand a number of words by nine months. When you chatter away to your grandbabies, you are stimulating future language.

And perhaps most important of all is the infants inborn desire to socialize, a fact that will become apparent from the first time they are in your arms. Crying is the first means of communication and researchers at Brown University have identified what you learned as a parent; that there are distinctly different cries of hunger, discomfort, and even a manufactured cry for attention when boredom sets in.

Left alone, all normal babies learn to talk, move, and learn, but they are giving powerful clues about their personalities by doing so at individual rates. Personality is a strong component of any child's behavior, even newborns, so tune in to their unique, individual preferences so you can respect and enjoy them from the start. These are the individual gifts that each grandchild will offer you.

Keep in mind that infancy is a fleeting stage that everyone in the family will want to enjoy to the fullest extent possible.

## Toddlers

Toddlers are still pretty much as you remember them; independent and headstrong. They are still likely to throw the same temper tantrums and to get into the same difficult moods when they are hungry or tired.

Fortunately, the approaches that worked for you before will still work now if you can muster the patience that it takes to employ them. The primary of these is to anticipate, anticipate, anticipate, all the time; trying to stay one step ahead of your toddler grandchildren. Anticipate nap times and get home before toddlers become overly tired and resist badly needed rest. Anticipate thirst, hunger, and toileting before discomfort hits. And when all else fails, dance a jig. A jig rarely fails to distract an out of sorts toddler!

There are still innate challenges to caring for toddlers, regardless of how good your approach is. They lack reasoning ability and have a tremendous drive to move and move and move. Safety needs to be on your mind all the time. Turning away for even a moment can result in a spilled cup of hot coffee, or a terrifying dash into the street to retrieve the child.

Another key strategy for toddlers is using touch as a soothing technique. Rocking, singing, hugging, lifting, and kissing send strong body language messages to your preverbal toddler grandchildren and you can use them effectively as secret defenses.

Toileting is an issue that comes up during this period. Regardless of how you did it as a parent, you are wise to step back and take your cues from what the parents want to do. Even better, if asked for advice, consider a sudden lapse of memory on the subject.

The National Network for Child Care out of Iowa State University advises against early training (before age one year) as it is little more than catching what the child accidentally eliminates. Toilet training is different from any of the other tasks that the young child needs to learn and it requires a wide range of skills, such as language, small motor agility to get the pants down, and a cooperative personality. The latter is frequently lacking in the average two-year-old!

These abilities rarely occur before the age of eighteen months and sometimes don't appear until the child nears the third birthday. A child with disabilities may require even a later start.

One good way to be supportive is to offer to buy colorful cotton underwear designed just for training toddlers. Or, buy a potty chair for your home that looks like the one at the child's home.

Part of the challenge of toilet training stems from the high activity level of young children. As far as many toddlers are concerned, toileting is an interruption of their play that uses up too much precious time! Keep in mind (or be willing to share the thought) that there is nothing wrong with returning to diapers for a month or two if first tries are not successful.

Leave power struggles for the parents and child because you are off the hook this time! Enjoy your grandbaby, who will be grown up all too soon, leaving the whole question a nonissue.

## Preschoolers

The urge to move will remain a big challenge with preschool grandchildren as you try to cope with their incredibly high energy and activity levels. Grandparents have been known to wear themselves out trying to slow grandchildren down, but moving and playing are a passion and efforts to stop, rather than to channel, usually prove futile.

What might seem like excessive activity and short attention spans are quite common at this age. For preschoolers, there is simply so much to do and explore!

They have a difficult time waiting for anything, so strategies should center on avoiding situations where they can become bored or cranky. It also helps if you can keep interesting things on hand when you are out and about on errands. Vigorous outdoor play also helps to tame the abundant energy.

Unfortunately, dawdling is as much a part of preschool behavior as rushing is, but you're a grandparent now and you might be able to take dawdling in stride. Getting dressed is a prime target for both dawdling and control battles. Preschoolers know that dressing is important to adults and daily battles can brew unless you are willing to let them go out in orange stripes and plaids occasionally. Your best bet is to try to catch their imaginations and turn dressing (or any other chore, for that matter) into a game.

Tell your granddaughter that she is the red fairy and that she can only put on red clothes while you have to do the rest. Or, let your grandson see how many pieces of his clothing come in pairs. Have him count as he puts in two arms, two legs, two socks, etc.

Naps are another area that preschoolers will resist vigorously. If your own kids were good nappers, you might be puzzled at your grandchildren's reluctance. Some children are born nappers and others aren't. Sleeping traits are obvious in infancy and carry through in early childhood, even into adulthood. Trying to treat all grandchildren the same, where sleep is concerned, is bound to have mixed results. Since both the number and frequency of naps decreases with age, regardless of the innate pattern, the whole question will settle itself in a few years.

If you live near enough for frequent visits, the first request to spend the night will undoubtedly come during the preschool years. If you extend such an invitation, be prepared for the possibility of a middle of the night change of heart. Preschoolers are known for their bravado, but bedtimes are often difficult for them and some will not be able to sleep away from home for a few years to come. The best way to judge readiness is to consider your grandchild's overall personality.

Nightmares are common during the preschool years and they include visions of monsters and other horrible creatures. Monitoring bedtime television will help considerably because nightmares are the work of the child's unconscious mind. Telling reality from fantasy is still not easy, especially at night in the dark and away from home.

If you have preschool grandchildren sleeping over, it can help to guide them toward a regular bedtime routine that includes quiet activities, a bedtime snack, hygiene tasks, and the final ultimatum. If they remain hesitant, try using a small night-light.

## School-Age Children

Gone are the pudgy cheeks and protruding tummies. From now until about age ten, your grandchildren will appear on your doorstep with knees and long limbs covered with bruises. Girls and boys are about the same size, but those growth patterns will change shortly.

Your school-age grandchildren have gone from the nearly total dependence of early childhood to wanting to share a stake in their own control. Arguing is common, which can make this a difficult time of transition for everyone in the family.

As a grandparent, you are in an excellent position to understand and appreciate these changes. This is one of those times when your hindsight will prove most valuable. You know that rebellion and parental challenge lies ahead, but you will not generally be the target of this behavior and your close relationship should continue, unscathed.

A highly effective approach for working with these grandchildren is to offer them more and more choices when they spend time with you. They are fun companions and eager learners who love nothing better than to be moving, learning, and doing. Biking, hiking, swimming, and skating are high on their list of favorites, although competence at these things is spotty. No problem. That won't deter their enthusiasm, so take their attempts seriously when they are trying something that is difficult for them.

Tattling is one of many tools in the arsenal of annoying behaviors perfected by school-age children. The behavior can be more vengeful than informational, which makes it all the more annoying. As a grandparent, you are a perfect target if multiple grandchildren are competing for your attention. The thought of getting a sibling or cousin into trouble can be very tempting.

What can you do to keep from being the "meanie"? You can try to explain (again and again, as often as necessary) that there is a difference between reporting information and telling just to get someone in trouble. Express your displeasure with the latter. Go back over the problem with them and have them try to come up with solutions. This will take a little more of your time initially, but it can help you to avoid repetitions of tattling.

School-age grandchildren are a joy to be around. Given the opportunity, they have an amazing ability to think through their own problems and come up with solutions that are effective. They need lots of opportunities to practice emerging skills. Telling the child what to do all the time takes away golden opportunities. By taking the time necessary to listen to their problems and concerns, no matter how trivial they might sound to you at the time, you are encouraging them to look deep inside and find their own answers. Try asking them questions like the following when you want to put the burden where it belongs:

How do you feel about that?

What are you concerned about?

Can you think of some way to solve the problem?

What do you think he is feeling?

If you commit yourself to this slower method of investigation, you can be sure that your grandchildren have the opportunity to explore these valuable new life skills. The alternative is to do the reasoning for them because it saves time, a strategy that will ensure endless years of your having to dispense justice.

Give school-age grandchildren a relaxed and fertile environment to work in. Let them make dinner with you, or help you plant a tree, repair a bicycle, or shop for groceries. Let them show how they can run a computer or do a complex math problem. Their self-esteem will blossom!

# Adolescents

The last stages of childhood are frequently viewed as among the most challenging, but grandparents do not need to find them so. Somewhere between the knobby-kneed elementary school child and the smart and savvy high school student lies the awkward junior high school grandchild, begging you to assure them that everything will turn out fine.

For granddaughters, there has likely been rapid physical growth with an eye level view of you for the first time. With that can come the startling realization that childhood is coming to a close. Grandsons tend to be shorter and less physically developed than their female counterparts.

No junior high school grandchild is pleased with their own rate of physical development. When they are late maturing, they complain that they feel like babies among their peers. They can even have trouble competing in team sports with larger, stronger kids the same age. The boys are much shorter at this age, which adds insult to injury. If the child is early maturing there is still no real advantage as he or she is out of step with everyone for at least a few years.

Uneven bone and muscle growth can cause awkward appearances like temporarily large noses, protruding ears, and overly long arms; things that only grandparents can love and appreciate! Throw in a few cowlicks and pimples, a voice change, or the onset of menstruation and a grandchild can feel like the ugliest of ducklings.

Fortunately, grandparents know better! They know that adolescent grandchildren have to discover their sense of personal identity, and that they need to question many of the things that they have accepted until now. Somewhat comically (to the grandparent, not to the grandchild), they do so by adhering to strict hair and dress codes that make them look exactly like everyone else. The parents might be horrified, but in this case, the grandparent *has* seen it all and knows that it will pass.

Life for the junior high grandchild is pretty much like a roller coaster ride, with people like grandparents waving cheerfully as they race by. Some of them are amazingly mature, but most will lean in the other direction.

As the impartial and trusted outsider, grandparents have a definite advantage with their adolescent grandchildren. They can frequently give them sound advice when no one else in the family can. They can create welcome havens when there are conflicts at home, or when grandchildren feel rejected or misunderstood (as long as there is approval from the parents).

The junior high years are not all stormy. It is easy for parents to get caught up in superficial battles over hair and clothes, forgetting that the grandchild simply *cannot* be different from the crowd. Grandparents can enjoy the emerging reasoning abilities and challenge grandchildren with inquiries into life issues. This is a great time to imagine possibilities together.

## Teenagers

The high school years mark the final transition out of childhood and into adulthood. By now the grandparents know their grandchildren well and have a clear appreciation of their special abilities and interests. High school grandchildren will tell their grandparents anything they want to know if they are asked, although sometimes misguided idealism and enthusiasm appear.

Maturity levels vary, so some patience is still warranted if a grandchild isn't everything a grandparent wishes yet. A great deal of learning, discovery, and personal growth still lie ahead. Because the decisions that high school grandchildren make can affect their adult futures, they usually need the outside perspective of someone other than their parents.

Grandparents can be their biggest fans during these years, sharing in the enjoyment of their accomplishments, both big and small. A good grade on an algebra test is as worthy of celebration as a touchdown at the football game, and it can be shared across the distances if the grandparent is not nearby.

When teenage grandchildren make mistakes, grandparents can be there to listen and offer whatever assistance is appropriate, as long as it doesn't entail bailing them out of expensive mistakes that were the result of misjudgments. Grandparents know from experience that the most valuable part of the learning process is having to live with the consequences of chosen actions. This is an age when grandchildren can benefit from mistakes, as long as loving adults stand nearby.

## EXPLORING RULE 4 CONCEPTS

*Review the status of your attitudes about teaching and learning from grandchildren by asking yourself the following questions:*

1. **Can I think of three words to describe each grandchild's unique personality?**

*Always:*
- They are always on the tip of your tongue!
- Not only are they there, but they give you great pleasure.

*Sometimes:*
- Perhaps you know some grandchildren better than others. Is there a reason for that? Is there a solution?
- You may be trying to impose your ways of doing things on your grandchildren, which rarely works.
- Come up with at least one word for each of them, and work on refining that to include more.

*Never:*
- Look at some photographs of grandchildren and see what words come to mind.

## 2. Do I have grandchildren whose personalities clash with mine?

*Always:*
- A certain amount of this is normal. Your truthfulness should help you to accept and compensate for that reality.

*Sometimes:*
- The traits that you find annoying now could be assets in adulthood (persistence, high energy, talkativeness)!
- No problem—as long as you aren't acting on it.
- Maybe *your* personality is clashing with theirs!

*Never:*
- The odds of this are probably rare.

## 4. Can I list three things that I have learned from each grandchild?

*Always:*
- Foremost among them is patience!

*Sometimes:*
- Try harder to listen to what they try to share with you.
- Allow each grandchild to teach you something that they like to do (roll a ball, play pat-a-cake, read, work on the computer).
- Hug them as a reward!

*Never:*
- Become all eyes and ears!

## 5. Do I remember the basic developmental patterns of children?

*Always:*
- You must have done a refresher course. Continue to update your knowledge with current magazines, books, and Internet information.

*Sometimes:*
- Review so you can keep one step ahead as they change.
- Resist relying just on memory.
- Look into the stages that you don't know as much about.

*Never:*
- Pick up a good reference book, such as:
  *Your Child's Growing Mind* by Jane Healy
  *Caring for Your Baby & Young Child,* Schelov and Hannemann, eds.
  *Caring for Your School-Age Child,* Schor, ed.

## Rule 5:
# GRANDPARENTS SHOULD LOVE TO SPOIL

## SENSE AND SENSIBILITY

What greater pleasure is there than giving to grandchildren? When grandparents give, the joy felt is immeasurable and they will tell you so, to a grandparent! What possible reason could there be why that urge should be curtailed? Unfortunately, the urge to spoil is one that does need careful attention, for if it is done without purposeful goals in mind, it can have the opposite effect from that which is intended.

Reasonable grandparents know that too much of a good thing can stop being good, and spoiling can overcome good sense, common sense, and money sense.

The subject of spoiling is an emotionally charged one because it is impossible to tell precisely when enough is enough. On one side of the line the giving works great; on the other side, grandchildren become petulant, demanding and . . . well, spoiled! The challenge that you face with the spoiling rule is that you have to determine where that fine line is for each of your grandchildren, and it can vary from child to child.

> It might be hard to believe that something that feels so good can turn bad, but thus is born the most notorious of all grandparent rules; the one that makes good grandparents do foolish things, in the name of love.

If you accept the rule wholeheartedly and make no attempt to temper your giving with some advance direction, you can negatively impact a grandchild's behavior, despite your best intentions.

There is nothing wrong with wanting to give your grandchildren things that will make them happy. Most grandparents are grateful that they are able to give their grandchildren things that they could not afford for their own kids. Your grandchildren need to know that you love them and your well-thought-out spoiling can boost their self-esteem by showing them in tangible ways how special you know that they are!

Grandparents joke that spoiling is repayment for the years spent raising one's own children. If you want to spoil, you are in the good company of millions of other grandparents of like mind. But consider the unthinkable as you explore the logic and consequences of spoiling. What would happen if you broke this rule? What kind of a grandparent would you be if you decided not to spoil at every opportunity?

That idea of limiting spoiling can be frightening, for it frequently conjures up nasty words like *stingy*, *cranky*, and *tight*—certainly not words that you want applied to you as a grandparent!

The answer lies somewhere in between and you can discover what it means for you by experimenting and making careful observations as you give to your grandchildren. Spoiling is a valid activity, but it cannot be done in an unrestricted manner without causing some level of negative consequences; consequences that are as painful to your grandchildren as they are to you!

No grandparent wants their grandchildren to be demanding, rude, or ungrateful and that certainly isn't what is intended by their gifts. A loving grandparent needs to develop workable methods of spoiling that promotes the child's well-being.

Giving a reasonable amount of treats and gifts is part of the solution, although giving less will not automatically guarantee appreciation. Consider some of the suggestions below to get you started on developing levels of spoiling that work both for you, and for your grandchildren:

- **Give no more than two gifts at a time.** A good rule of thumb is to give one or two things at a time (even for birthdays) so your grandchildren can learn to focus on what they have received instead of on what is coming next. It can overwhelm young children if they receive too many gifts at one time.

- **Let grandchildren choose a gift or goodie.** Putting limits on giving could also mean telling your grandchildren that they can select one item from the many that they want when they are out shopping with you. Making choices encourage decision-making abilities (because they will guess wrong sometimes) and delayed gratification, both of which are important life skills for children to develop.

- **Make sure that you always give something of yourself with every gift.** That could mean taking the time to sit down together when you give a cookie so that you can dunk it into milk together. Or, it could mean lying on your back on the grass to gaze up at the new kite you have given. It means helping grandchildren to figure out the instructions to the new board game, or rolling the ball back and forth to a toddler.

- **Don't overload at birthdays and holidays.** Consider spreading your toy giving throughout the year instead of overwhelming your grandchildren at Christmas or on their birthdays. Children need variety in playthings all year because of their short attention spans.

- **Rotate the toys at your home.** Variety doesn't have to mean new. Interest in an old toy can be renewed if it is put away for a while and brought out again. If you don't want your grandchildren to relate to you primarily as a gift giver, you need to give sparingly, thoughtfully, and (generally) unpredictably. You may want to consider supplementing store purchases with things you have around the house like you did when you were a young parent on a budget. Remember how much your babies loved the boxes, wrapping, and bows; sometimes even more than what was inside?

- **Say "no" sometimes.** Giving wisely can mean saying "no" sometimes, even when you can afford what your grandchildren want, and even though you want to buy it for them. If children know that grandparents always give them what they want, they cannot focus on the giving, but only on the receiving. Giving is an act of love because it is a decision to express love, not because of the object that is given.

If your love and attention accompany occasional refusals to buy, you'll be surprised how quickly grandchildren will get over their disappointment and move on. And if they don't get over it quickly, it's more important than ever to stick to your guns and put a hold on giving, for if it is done without purposeful goals in mind, it can have the opposite effect. Try showering them with gifts of time, phone calls, letters, or postcards until you have broken patterns of unreasonable expectations.

By not always agreeing to buy things, you can help grandchildren focus away from objects and onto your attentions to them. They can experience the good feelings that result from personal interchanges as much as the joy of a new toy or treat. Try telling your grandchildren that you don't have enough money to buy toys today, but you would like to take them to the park to feed the ducks. You won't be disappointed with the results.

Children who don't get exactly what they want may suffer some degree of initial disappointment. If they get a more appropriate gift like a set of blocks for construction, or a set of hand puppets for pretend play, they will eventually forget their disappointment, especially if grandparents get down on the floor to join the fun.

- **Resist manipulation. Children are experts at it!** It is important to resist the insidious fear that grandchildren will think they are unloved if they don't get exactly what they want. What grandparent wants to risk that? Fortunately, grandparent-grandchild love is built on a bond of love more constant than that. Gifts are only one small expression of that love. The real value lies in teaching grandchildren about the beauty of giving and receiving, which is sometimes diminished by media advertising that make youngsters demand too much.
- **Buy out of love, not to get love.** A good rule of thumb to follow when you buy toys is to make sure that you are purchasing out of love and not to get love. There is nothing wrong with enjoying the pleasure your grandchildren experience when they receive gifts, but your pleasure will be even greater if they are still using and enjoying your gift a month after they received it because it is an appropriate toy, or because you have enjoyed it in some way together.

# PARENT REACTIONS

Do parents need to be consulted when you want to give? This is an area fraught with possible repercussions if you choose to ignore it. Generally speaking, giving to your grandchildren should be your choice and should not have to be limited by parents, as long as you aren't going overboard. However, if parents express concerns that your spoiling is causing undesirable behavior changes, they do have a right to ask you to modify what you are doing.

Very real jealousy can arise from the spoiling that well-meaning grandparents do. Knowing that they cannot compete on the same level as you can cause resentment, even though they are happy that their children are enjoying your gifts. Parents sometimes feel that the gifts they give are less appreciated by their children, putting them in direct competition with you for their love and attention.

> Parents want to give their children the best, but when they do not have the resources to do so, they can feel bad. When the grandparents give more than Santa, something is wrong!

In moderation, and in concert with loving attention, spoiling accomplishes good ends. It is always healthy to make children feel special. Spoiling is positive when it strengthens children's self-esteem and makes them feel worthwhile to the adults who matter in their lives.

You can glean a great deal of pleasure by knowing that your grandchildren will be delighted with a surprise, instead of having them waiting with open hands every time you are around. Besides, if grandchildren are looking for a handout, they aren't looking for hugs, and which would you rather give? The choice is yours to make.

# SUGAR AND SPICE

If you have developed unhealthy eating habits over the years, grandchildren give you an opportunity to shed those habits in their best interests. By about nine months, children begin to take an interest in what is on *your* plate. What they find there could profoundly influence their later food choices. Hopefully they can find fresh fruits and vegetables instead of potato chips and French fries.

Treats and goodies comprise a major area of grandparent giving. Unfortunately, many children need their grandparents to exercise care in this area for they are growing up on fast food, shakes, and sodas.

Research at the Mayo Clinic confirms that hardened, thickened arteries (atherosclerosis) originates in childhood. Fatty deposits in children's arteries are becoming alarmingly common.

Unless you are the daily baby-sitter, you may have little control over daily eating habits, but you can set a good example of nutritious eating whenever your grandchildren are with you. This doesn't mean that you can't offer an occasional sweet or cookie, but encouraging proper nutrition doesn't have to be unpleasant. It could be one of the kindest things that you ever do for your grandchildren.

A bottomless cookie jar teaches children always to expect sweet treats instead of the wide variety of choices of healthy snacks. If you load up on sugary treats for your grandchildren, you are liable to finish them yourself when they go home!

Snacks can make up to 20% of a young child's daily food intake because most young children have a difficult time eating enough food at one meal to last until the next one. Because snacks play such a major nutritional role, offering junk food robs children of opportunities for nutrients and vitamins that they need.

Snack foods do not need to be banned; they need to be planned! Little bodies need proper fueling to avoid energy crashes and crabby moods and the kinds of empty calories found in junk foods rob them of needed nutrients.

Wouldn't a homemade oatmeal raisin cookie create a much nicer memory than a packaged cupcake? And what about cubes of cheese on little colored toothpicks instead of a packaged marshmallow cookie with a shelf life of twelve months? If you are eating bread sticks, bagels, grapes, and frozen yogurt, your grandchildren will want them, too. And while you are at it, why not consider eliminating processed, packaged, and convenience foods for your grandchildren altogether? They may be easier to serve, but they don't offer valuable lessons about nutrition.

All it takes is the ability to run against consumer brainwashing so that you can spoil your grandchildren in a smarter and far more loving way. If your grandchildren never eat processed or junk foods at your house, they won't come looking for them when you visit. And who knows? They could end up actually looking forward to the unusual kinds of treats that you always have to offer them!

# "NO FAIL" TOY SELECTIONS

Buying gifts and toys is another area where spoiling can overcome good sense. Once grandparents can accept the fact that the price paid does not equal toy value, they will be on their way toward focusing more correctly on what they are giving. Making "no-fail" toy purchases is easy if some of these suggestions are followed:

- **Pay attention to the age suggested on the box.**   Suggested ages on toy packages are generally good indicators of developmental appropriateness. Challenging a grandchild with something designed for an older child is not a way to accelerate learning!
- **Be reasonable with what you spend.**   A high price does not guarantee a good toy. There is no correlation between the two, so always look for quality materials instead of a flashy name.
- **Look for toys that are multipurpose.**   Developmentally appropriate toys can be used for more than one thing. Good examples are imaginative toys like blocks, dolls, trucks.
- **Buy only sturdy toys.**   No matter how much your grandchildren nag you for junk, stick to high-quality materials.
- **Look for toys that can be used alone or with someone else.** When a child needs someone to play with in order to use a toy, it can be frustrating. Toys that can be used either way are more useful.
- **Try to buy at least some toys that can be used by children of either sex.**
- **Look for toys that require the child to think and engage in pretend play.**

# SETTING UP A PLAY ENVIRONMENT

Having the right toys on hand for visiting grandchildren is important because it can eliminate most, if not all, fighting, arguing, and boredom. Storing playthings where the grandchildren can get to them easily by themselves also encourages them to clean up when they are done.

You don't need a whole separate playroom to accomplish these goals. A portable laundry basket, a hall closet, or a kitchen cupboard all work equally well. As far as "educational toys" go, consider toy labeling as you would other labeling; the consumer is frequently given more innuendo than fact!

Why would any self-respecting toy company label their products any other way? Educational is what sells. The word holds strong consumer appeal and enables toy companies to compete effectively for your toy dollars.

The problem with this concept is that it only tells you half of the truth.

There is nothing intrinsic in educational toys that makes them learning tools. The teaching part is in the adult attention that reinforces the child's attraction to the toy.

A toy can make a child curious, but it cannot teach. It is of little value until the adult enters into the play. The child learns when there is a meaningful interaction with a caring adult and that is where you can come in!

# THE PLAYFUL GRANDPARENT

It is important to understand why children play when you shop for toys. Shopping in a toy store today is an intimidating walk through seemingly limitless choices, none of which resemble the things you remember buying.

Then again, maybe the very idea of sitting down and playing scares you. Maybe you think you have forgotten how to play, or perhaps you didn't have the time to do it with your own children when they were young so that it feels uncomfortable.

Playing with grandchildren is spoiling at its best! Being a grandparent gives you a wonderful second opportunity to do it all over again the right (and playful) way!

Play comes naturally to children and they will always welcome you into their fun if you show a willingness to suspend a few of your (unplayful) adult behaviors. All that you need to get you started is love for your grandchildren and a desire to share in and enjoy their adventures.

Play is like love; everyone does it, but it is still difficult to define. Research by neuroanatomists shows that the cerebral cortex of the brain (the area largely concerned with thinking) responds to play somewhat like muscles respond to exercise, growing larger and stronger in every dimension. Animals that play are among the more intelligent of the species. The human child has the longest dependent period of any species and that appears to be directly connected to its higher intelligence.

Play for children might be loosely defined as everything that they do when they aren't busy getting their basic needs (eating, sleeping) met. There is no universal standard by which it can be measured, and what is fun for one child might not be fun for another. Personality plays a large role in play choices. You can play with a baby and you can play with a teenager. (Play is even making a considerable comeback among senior citizens!)

When you think back to your own childhood, the kinds of activities that filled your free time were probably far different from what you see your grandchildren doing. Your time was probably spent roaming through the neighborhood, farm, or city with only your imagination to guide you. Your forts were trees and your theaters were folding chairs. Restaurants and lemonade stands sprang from lumber scraps and cardboard boxes.

Today, many children play in organized group activities like child care, music lessons, scouts, and team sports. Their play goals are the same: relaxation, exercise, and creativity, to name a few. What they frequently lack is play that challenges their imaginations, which is something that you can work on when you are together.

Pretend play allows young children to experience and act out things that are puzzling or frightening to them. It also lets them experience the bizarre and impossible. It brings laughter and enjoyment and an escape from reality.

What a pleasant surprise it would be for your grandchildren to find out that Grandma and Grandpa like to pretend, too! No one told you how to pretend when you were a child up in a tree, but your grandchildren might need assistance. They might not be used to being inventive and carefree in their play.

A good way to stimulate pretend play is to introduce prop boxes into the fun. Both boys and girls will enjoy a box full of hats, shoes, purses, jewelry, and wigs. Add card tables, chairs, and blankets and you can help them build a royal carriage, a speeding train, a cozy home, or a busy office.

Most important of all, you can be a role model and show a little silliness so your grandchildren get into the spirit of things. Become one of the characters and get the imaginations cranking. Use provoking questions to sustain the game. For instance, if you are going on a train ride ask your grandchildren where they want to go, who else is riding along, and why they are heading for their chosen destination.

When they get the idea, you can encourage them to help you put together additional pretend play boxes that are ready and waiting for them whenever they come to visit. Consider some of the following suggestions and see where they lead you:

*Office Kit*

   calculator

   pads of paper

   unplugged telephone

   junk mail

   rubber stamps and ink pad

   pens

   stapler

   sorting boxes or trays

*Restaurant Kit*

   empty food boxes

   menus

   play money

   aprons

   music

   pens and small pads for menus

   dishes and silverware

*Radio Station*

   tape deck

   assorted tapes

   glasses, hats

   paper and pens

   microphone

*Travel Agency*

   travel brochures

   travel posters

   pads and pens

   unplugged telephone

   calculator

   old airline tickets

# THE PLAYFUL CHILD

Play is a child's way of learning about the world. As a grandparent, you can initiate successful play every time you are with your grandchildren if you present play opportunities that are developmentally appropriate.

If you are using a purchased toy, make sure that it is rated by age. If you are using your own materials, the following developmental readiness guidelines can help you to stay on target. Then, you can spoil your grandchildren with hours of enjoyable play that will enhance your time together.

## Infants

Newborns and infants play as a means of gathering basic information about the world. Play is also critical in allowing them to build attachments to the significant adults in their lives as they play with them.

The natural attraction that adults have to babies furthers this effort. When they play, adults naturally act in unusual ways in order to catch and hold a baby's attention, yet few of them ever feel uncomfortable using silly, high-pitched voices and exaggerated movements.

Infant play is also useful for promoting physical development, encouraging curiosity, and making the world more predictable through hands-on experience.

## Toddlers

Toddlers are on the move and their play is exploration. The primary task is still the same; gathering information about the world. Playthings that encourage them to move about are good choices. The mouth is the primary exploration tool, and that means that everybody needs to be on alert to safety.

*Playthings for infants and toddlers*
Basic play supplies are easy to find for your youngest grandchildren because much of what you need is right in your home, especially in your kitchen. Purchasing expensive play equipment for babies is unnecessary. They are curious explorers and they will latch on to whatever they find, or that you provide. Try pulling out some of the items suggested below and watch your grandbabies gurgle with glee:

cans
large spoons and spatulas

pots and pans with lids
egg cartons
milk cartons
paper (newspaper, wrapping paper, shelf paper; **never** plastic bags)
shoes
large beaded necklaces
hats
bright scarves
empty boxes
finger foods (toddlers)

If you wish to purchase some additional supplies for grandbabies, stick to basic favorites and rotate them for novelty and variety, both of which are very important. Any of the following will get you plenty of mileage for your money:

balls of all sizes and colors
soft plastic toys
soft dolls without hair or button eyes
sturdy books
plastic keys
plastic play telephone
musical toys and music boxes

## Ages Two and Three

Twos and threes have pretty much mastered basic movement and it is likely that they will never sit still. Their fingers are the tool of choice, replacing (but not eliminating) the mouth for exploring the world.

These children love to pull things apart and put them back together again. Successful play will usually include that emerging skill in some way. They run about like little physicists, experimenting on everything that they can get their hands on, and your home will always end up in a state of clutter when they visit. You might as well get down there on the floor with them and enjoy the inevitable but necessary mess that is a part of having them around.

*Playthings for twos and threes*
There are still many common household items that will keep these grandchildren entertained. Because language is in full bloom, books

will be among their favorites if you read to them. They will usually insist that you read the same story over and over again. Another favorite activity is dumping and filling, a messy but enjoyable way to spend the time. Don't forget some art supplies for these beginning scribblers and budding artists. Things you may already have on hand include:

kitchen utensils
purses (to empty and fill)
hats, shoes, shirts, and nightgowns
books with large colored pictures
pencils, pens, felt pens (at the table)
sponges, plastic tubs, vegetable brushes, etc., for water play.

If you want to supplement this list, avoid fad toys advertised on television as these grandchildren won't know the difference. Purchase durable, tried-and-true items like these for better results:

picture storybooks
balls
dolls
art supplies
small garden tools
plastic tea and cooking sets
three-wheeled riding toys
trucks for dumping sand and mud
bucket type tree swing
small wagon, wheelbarrow
simple five- and six-piece puzzles
small cars
small blocks
plastic lunch pail
toy telephone

## Ages Four and Five

These are great ages for play and these grandchildren want to do it from the moment they open their eyes in the early morning until the end of each day when they drop from exhaustion.

Motor skills are strong with lots of running and climbing, which makes parks and the outdoors popular. Language is fluent and imagination and pretend play are at high levels. What fun playmates they can be for you! They make great companions and are full of questions as their minds move about as quickly as their bodies.

*Playthings for ages four and five*
You can still get away with using household items if you add a level of complexity. For example, give more props for water play or add a block set to go along with the trucks and cars. Pretend play is a favorite with this age and pretend works best with a few simple items. Help them to build tents with chairs and sheets and provide dress-up clothes to encourage playacting of all sorts. If there is a beginning interest in writing, have the tools they need on hand. Things to collect from around the house include:

mud, sand, water
large empty boxes to crawl into
pouring and measuring tools
rice, beans, and water for the above tools
drawing paper
art supplies
first scissors
dough
empty bottles and water
dress-up clothes
real (small) hammers with large-headed nails
insect collecting jars

The pressure to buy toys that are advertised on television is in full force now. There are many good developmentally appropriate alternates that have stood the test of time. Consider some of the following to spend your toy dollars on:

more art and craft supplies
balls
jump rope
kite
used bike
adventure books

blocks and construction sets (Tinkertoys, Legos)
Frisbee
story records and tapes
croquet set
twenty- to thirty-piece puzzles
dough, clay
needles, thread, buttons, fabric

## Ages Six to Nine

This is the age when involvement in team sports begins. Running and climbing no longer provide enough of a challenge and there is a fascination with grown-up equipment like bats, balls, hoops, and skates. What these grandchildren lack in coordination is made up for by a zest, drive, and the sheer willpower to learn and to master.

## Ages Ten to Twelve

The world of the preteen is expanding and growing in complexity. Competitiveness is at a high level and team sports are taken very seriously, often consuming much of their leisure time. Fostering an interest in sports and physical activities can help to stem the social tide, which is beginning to flow toward the opposite sex.

These grandchildren have an unbridled enthusiasm for anything that they are involved in and they love adults to participate with them and show them how to do new things.

*Playthings for school-age children, ages six to twelve*
By now you have a good idea of each grandchild's personality and of the things you enjoy doing together. Gone are the days when it was a full-time job to keep them busy. Now your time together can be focused on things that you both enjoy doing, including some of the following:

cooking supplies
garden tools
mud, sand, and water
photo albums
tools and discarded appliances (to take apart after the plugs are
  cut off)
woodworking tools

playing cards
sewing supplies
insect collecting jars
tree swing or house
containers for collecting just about anything

School-age grandchildren are ready for the challenge of extended projects that can be spread out over days, weeks, or even months. They are also fond of materials that can help them master new skills. Kits are one good example of this.

How wonderful to enjoy the less hurried and more grown-up level of interaction that now happens with these grandchildren? Suggested additional purchases include any of the following:

adventure books
taped stories
Legos, construction sets
art supplies (lots)
rubber stamps
car and airplane kits
magnifying glass
telescope
hammer and nails
sewing kit
children's cookbooks
sports equipment (used is fine)
used bike
board games
kite
aquarium
materials to make a garden scarecrow

## Teens

Whoever says that teenagers are impossible to be with is not a grandparent! Teens are more fun than ever to play with for they are eager to share themselves when adults are willing to listen and accept them. Ask them about their music, ideas, magazines, and fashions, and if you are willing to pay attention you will get an earful.

Bikes and basketballs are still appreciated, although they will probably be displaced by activities like eating and sleeping, which will begin to take up a frustrating amount of your precious visiting time.

*Fun things for teenagers*
These grandchildren are almost adults now and you can enjoy their company in whole new ways. Even though they think they are grown-up, you know that they still need love and attention and a suggestion for something to do once in a while. Fortunately, there are still a few things around your house that can fit the bill:

cards
maps, travel brochures
books
cooking materials
tools
needlework
woodwork
sewing
photo albums
old things you have stored away
old clothes

If you want to buy something a little more special to have on hand, try some of the sure winners below that you can all enjoy together:

complex puzzles
board games
science kits
joke books
magazines
books of puzzles (crosswords, mazes, etc.)
Legos (yes, still!)

# GIVING MONEY TO GRANDCHILDREN

A discussion of spoiling would not be complete without a discussion of giving grandchildren money. As you have seen by working your way through the ideas in this rule, there are many ways to show your grandchildren that you love them. Contributing to their futures financially is one of many ways to show love if it is something that you want to do.

A good education, job skills training, or just starting adult life away from home are costly endeavors today and should continue to be so in the foreseeable future. Regardless of the ages of your grandchildren, there are relatively painless measures that you can take early on to help you realize financial priorities for them.

Some grandparents want to contribute to their grandchildren's college education and beginning to save early on is the key. Savings begun early in the child's life will compound and maximize your efforts tremendously. The wisest course of action to take is to consult a certified financial planner or accountant so that you can get the full advantage of tax breaks and learn about any new laws that will make saving more effective, even if you are only able to contribute a small amount like $25 to $50 a month.

Seed money for a purpose other than college, with your grandchild matching your contribution at a certain rate, is another good way to spark incentive and teach the value of money and savings. You might want to underwrite part of a home loan down payment, or home expansion for a newly married grandchild, or when a new baby is on the way. If travel with grandchildren has always been a goal, consider savings just for that purpose so you can create some memorable experiences together.

# WHEN ALL IS SAID AND DONE

When you are willing to examine this rule thoughtfully, and you have taken the time necessary in order to determine your priorities in giving time, talent, money, gifts, or anything else, the results will amaze you.

Spoiling is a wonderful thing for grandparents to do! Children remember these acts of love and kindness far into adulthood. Spoiling is the ultimate training in giving of one's self and of one's possessions when it is done correctly, and for the right reasons.

Proper spoiling trains grandchildren to understand and appreciate what they receive. Proper spoiling also reinforces for grandparents that they are on the right track and that what they are doing is having a positive effect on their grandchildren. This enhances the enjoyment inherent in spoiling for everyone!

## EXPLORING RULE 5 CONCEPTS

*The following questions can help you to design a plan of how, why, and when to spoil:*

## 1. Do I give to grandchildren because it feels good to me?

*Always:*
- Red flags should be waving!
- You should expect to be greeted with upturned hands instead of hugs and kisses.

*Sometimes:*
- Occasional slipups will occur, but keep them occasional.
- Regular slipups indicate a lack of commitment to the ideas in this rule.
- Work to focus on the quality of your time together.

*Never:*
- They probably beg you for stories, games, and hugs!

## 2. Do I give in order to be loved?

*Always:*
- The discovery of being loved for who you can be far more rewarding.

*Sometimes:*
- Grandchildren remember childhood possessions vaguely, if at all.
- A child's love can only be earned when there is an interpersonal exchange.
- Gifts and goodies bring momentary excitement, but so does a butterfly, a reflecting puddle, and a spider spinning a web.

*Never:*
- You understand the true meaning of love and you teach your grandchildren to do the same!

## 3. Do I buy more than is reasonable, or that I can afford?

*Always:*
- An examination of self-control may be in order.

*Sometimes:*
- Forgive yourself and try harder next time.
- Gather a box of "toys" from around your house, or the child's (as suggested in this rule) the next time you visit. You might be surprised by the result!
- Set a reasonable budget for grandchild items and stick to it. If you underspend one month, carry it over to the next as a reward for resisting impulse buying.

*Never:*
- Lucky grandchildren. You are giving them your best!

### 4. Do I know what each grandchild's favorite toy is?

*Always:*
- You are a playful grandparent.
- You are also alert to grandchildren's personalities and you respect their choices as a part of that.

*Sometimes:*
- Encourage them to tell you what they love by listening to them when they want your attention.
- If they are old enough, ask them. Also, be sure to ask them why it is their favorite.
- Remember that when a child loves something they want to do it again, and again, and again . . .

*Never:*
- Sit down on the floor and ask them what they would like to do. If they cannot talk yet, sit and wait and they will show you!

### 5. Do I always make time to play when I give a new gift?

*Always*
- You know the secret of gift-giving fun!

*Sometimes:*
- Avoid dropping off gifts until you do have time to play.
- Make sure that you are not giving for the wrong reasons. (See questions 1 and 2.)

*Never:*
- You are telling grandchildren that you are too busy for them.
- You are too busy for them.

### 6. Am I comfortable with normal play clutter?

*Always*
- You know the difference between clutter and dirt.
- You can get past adult standards in order to let children play and learn.

*Sometimes:*
- As long as it is at *their* home!
- As long as it gets put away from time to time.
- As long as there is a system for putting things away that makes sense to children (containers to store different kinds of toys, low accessible toy storage, no dump-it-all-in-one toy box).

*Never:*
- Fine, but keep it to yourself!

## 7. Do I model good eating habits for my grandchildren?

*Always:*
- You obviously have a strong commitment to good nutrition.

*Sometimes:*
- Congratulate yourself for the times that you succeed and keep working on the rest.
- Enroll in a nutrition class or read a good book so you understand why this makes sense!
- Identify one treat that grandchildren beg for and make a list of five healthy alternatives. For example, instead of potato chips give bread sticks, baked potato chips, toasted bagel, cracker, or muffin.

*Never:*
- Seek help! Read *The Complete Idiot's Guide to Smart Eating,* by Joy Bauer.

## Rule 6:

# GRANDPARENTS SHOULD BE FULL OF FUN IDEAS

## SO, WHY DON'T I REMEMBER THEM?

This is the rule that casts you into the role of social director. As the social director, your job is to make sure that your grandchildren are continually amused, entertained, diverted, and joyful. You are so much fun to be with that they cry when they have to leave you. Behind the whole issue lurks an insidious threat: Grandchildren who don't have fun won't want to come back again!

How does one live up to the ideal of the totally fun grandparent? It is entirely possible that you have long since forgotten how to play with children and that you might need a little help getting started again. Perhaps the best approach is to admit to yourself that the entertaining-grandparent ideal can be intimidating and that it is fine to seek out help when you need it.

There is nothing wrong with experiencing a twinge (or more) of fear when grandchildren come to visit! The worst stance you could take is to bluff your way through visits so that they end up leaving you exhausted and your home in shambles.

A busy kid is a happy kid, but given the fact that you are a grandparent, it is logical to assume that you are out of practice in the area of keeping kids happy. It has been a long time since children played at

86

your home, or depended on you to know what they should be doing every fifteen (or so) minutes.

Certainly, keeping grandchildren busily engaged when they are in your care will always be one of your greatest grandparent challenges, but that doesn't mean that you aren't willing, or able, to relearn. A little refresher course can get you back to managing the challenging world of young children in no time.

The suggestions contained in this rule are designed to help you get busy having the kind of fun with your grandchildren that you have waited a lifetime for. If you are willing to be a playful grandparent, you can master this rule and have more fun than you ever imagined along the way!

To help you select appropriately, a broad range of activity ideas are listed by the child's age, the level of energy expended, and the length of time that the activity is (realistically) likely to last.

Each grandchild has a unique personality and needs, which are helpful to take into account as you plan activities. For example, it is wise to give highly active grandchildren plenty of physical choices, building in quiet activities from time to time to keep them (and you!) from becoming overtired. For grandchildren who are more sedate, you can plan an art project, or read favorite stories together.

# MAKING YOUR HOME
# A FUN PLACE TO BE

Visits with your grandchildren will allow you to create memories and to get to know their individual personalities better. Visits also create opportunities to demonstrate what you believe is important for grandchildren to learn.

Visits shouldn't mean all pampering, although a certain amount of that will thrill grandchildren. Chores can be fun when they are meaningful tasks and when you treat your grandchildren as if they are able to handle them. Washing dishes in a sink filled with bubbles can provide a thoroughly enjoyable experience to a child, as can scrubbing the dinner vegetables with a stiff brush.

If the idea of putting your grandchildren to work makes you fearful that they will resist and hate to come back and visit, you can relax. Nothing could be further from the truth. Three sound child development principles come into play when it comes to assigning chores:

Children love spending time with attentive adults.

Children like to feel needed and important.

Children love tasks that are "grown-up" (even toddlers!)

Because well-planned chores that are age appropriate meet all of these criteria, even ordinary household work can become exciting to do. Participating with you in your day-to-day activities also helps your grandchildren to get to know you better because it promotes the kind of idle chatter that naturally happens when hands are busy. Working side by side also lets you demonstrate the pride that you take in completing a job.

The age appropriate chore suggestions below can help you to get started. It doesn't matter which task you choose, as long as you begin, engage, and finish it *together!*

## CHORES FOR GRANDCHILDREN

*Ages 2 to 4*

pick up toys

empty trash cans

help set table

sort items (silverware, laundry, etc.)

*Ages 5 to 6*

put away groceries

make beds

feed pets

put away shoes, magazines, newspapers, etc.

set and clear table

close drawers, closets, cupboards

*Ages 7 to 8*

sweep floors

make simple lunches

rake leaves

walk dog

vacuum

help with supervised cooking

*Ages 9 to 11*

wash car
prepare simple recipes
fold and put away laundry
straighten room

*Ages 12+*

mow lawns
hose down patio and walkways
run errands
do laundry
plan menus
prepare more complex recipes

# DAY VISITS

Single-day visits offer the best of all possible combinations. There is time to enjoy being together and to do something fun, and you get to relax at the end of the day when your grandchildren head home.

For day visits to be special, a certain amount of planning is required because it is easy to underestimate young children's needs so that they can get cranky or bored. You will be reminded of that from the moment that your grandchildren enter your door and the wild race begins!

If you live near your grandchildren, they probably visit regularly already. Living nearby allows you to do things together on a casual basis and enables a level of comfort to evolve. Your grandchildren know where things are and how to make themselves at home. Unfortunately, even this closeness and predictability won't slow down their activity levels, or stretch out their attention spans.

If you don't live near your grandchildren, you probably have to make do with occasional visits, which give you a chance to update yourself with their growth and the changes that have taken place since the last time you were together. As grandchildren get older, visits tend to occur near holidays or during summer vacations and other school breaks.

Unless the visit is precipitated by an emergency, you can have just the right activities and exactly the right play equipment assembled before they arrive.

It is easy to be fooled by the seeming simplicity of the single-day visit, but in spite of the short length of the stay, it is still important not to leave things to chance.

When planning your perfect day visit, remember that a key ingredient will always be flexibility. If your grandchildren become excited with a new idea that interrupts something you planned, acknowledge their idea, even if it means canceling something you have put effort into planning. View your plans as resources that are there to draw upon when grandchildren become restless or bored. If a swarm of butterflies invades your yard, enjoy them instead of heading into the kitchen to make cookies just because it is on your planning schedule.

Charting all of your activities ahead of time on a sheet like the one following can be helpful in keeping things running smoothly. Make sure to list common activities like meals and chores along with special outings and projects.

In your overall planning for any visit, it is important to aim for balance. If you alternate activities that are quiet and busy, you will have a better chance of controlling the difficult behaviors that can result from overstimulation. You knew the importance of naps and winding down before bedtime when you were a parent. The same goes with the grandchildren. It is up to you to build in the controls that allow you and your grandchildren to enjoy a workable and pleasant pace.

Another good strategy for increasing the fun with each visit is to make notes afterward about how your plans went. You will make mistakes and you will have successes. Your notes can prove invaluable for planning future visits, particularly with individual grandchildren whose behavior might be challenging.

If adults are staying for the visit, they will want to spend at least some of their time in adult conversation. This is when things can become difficult for the grandchildren, for it is unfair to invite grandchildren over only to have them spend the hours being told to go away and be quiet. That is *not* the kind of grandparent memories that you want to create.

One solution can be to plan for time when adults and children can interact together. That time could include a family game like charades where everyone (even toddlers) can participate. Family storytelling is another good activity that everyone can enjoy and enter into. Afterward, activities can be set up in another area of the house just for the children, with the adults taking turns facilitating those activities so that the others can talk uninterrupted. In that way, the children can get the attention they need to make their visit enjoyable.

**DAY VISIT PLAN**

Grandchild's Name:

Date:

| | Activity | Level | Time | Result |
|---|---|---|---|---|
| **MORNING** | bake muffins | quiet | 1/2 hr. | They ate them for breakfast and raved about them! |
| | wash dishes | moderate | 1/2 hr. | One washed and one dried. They sang songs as they worked. |
| | market | moderate | 1 hr. | Picked vegetables for dinner. |
| | park/picnic | active | 2 hrs. | They ran and ran! |
| **AFTERNOON** | stories/rest | quiet | 1 1/2 hrs. | They fell asleep. |
| | water play | active | 1 1/2 hrs. | Used buckets, hoses, funnels, spray bottles, etc. |
| | video/snack | quiet | 1 1/2 hrs. | Spread out the sleeping bags. |
| **EVENING** | dinner | quiet | 1 hr. | Helped prepare and loved the vegetables! |
| | walk | moderate | 1 hr. | Walked to get yogurt for dessert. |
| | cut fabric | quiet | 1 hr. | Will use scraps for an art project next visit. |
| | Sent home! | | | Quiet time for me!! |

91

It is relatively easy to manage and enjoy grandchildren when they are busy doing things that they enjoy. Relying on the toys they bring along with them rarely works, as children naturally seek novelty. It doesn't take long for grandchildren to become bored with their own belongings and then they will begin to look for new things to do.

Suggestions are provided later in this rule for activities to use when you are filling out your day visit plan and you need some new ideas. These exciting activities will help to assure that your grandchildren are not only busy, but that they are having the time of their lives!

# PLANNING FOR A LONGER STAY

A week with grandchildren can be a highlight in your relationship if you are realistically prepared for the ups, downs, and occasional strains of spending a great deal of time together. Visits of a week or longer take a good deal of planning and should never be taken lightly, even if they involve older grandchildren or teenagers. Your satisfaction is as much at stake in these visits as your grandchildren's.

## Dry Runs

If your grandchildren live nearby, you have probably had a few overnight visits already so that this will be more or less an extension of what has come before. If grandchildren are coming from out of town, it will be helpful if you can make things somewhat familiar for them by telling them about some of the things they will be seeing and doing during their stay. If they have never visited your home, you might consider sending photographs and descriptions of your surroundings.

## Ages

The ages of your grandchildren are important in making visits go smoothly, particularly if the parents are leaving your grandchildren alone with you. If there is a range of ages, the planning should take that into consideration.

Young children do best when prepared for new situations so that they know what to expect and can feel safe and comfortable. Most children under age five will experience some difficulty in visiting for more than a day or two, but these difficulties aren't insurmountable. It helps if at least one parent is around in the beginning of the stay to help younger children get settled before the visit continues alone. Older grandchildren will generally act more independently, and will be happier if they have some say about activity choices.

Whatever the ages of the visiting grandchildren, you can help everyone to enjoy themselves more by making sure that quality quiet time to be alone with each grandchild together is built in, for that is the purpose of visiting. Visits should include plenty of time to hug and touch, snuggle and cuddle. There should be time for spoiling and experiencing the special kind of love that only a grandparent can offer. While you can build a relationship by mail or phone, it is much more likely to happen when you are physically together, sharing good times.

## Personality

Personalities play heavily in the success of long visits. If you have not had the opportunity to spend a great deal of time together, it is helpful to ask the parents specific questions about the grandchildren's likes and dislikes in foods, habits, and activities. In that way, you can make things more comfortable when they arrive.

Some children have no trouble being away from their parents, but others feel uncomfortable in any new situation. Some children are easily occupied, and others have short attention spans, are overly talkative, or have other personal habits that can annoy even the most loving of grandparents.

Personality traits can be appreciated more readily if you remember to view each child as an individual, and to plan things specifically to meet their needs.

## Activities

Some children are resourceful when it comes to finding things to fill their time, but most youngsters need some adult help and direction. Remember the long summers that you spent with your own kids listening to that dreaded refrain, "There's nothing to do!"

Begin your activity planning by sketching out a framework for a week at a time, using a planner like the one following. Ask your friends where they take their grandchildren when they visit and scan the papers for low-cost community events. Short excursions are preferable to full-day outings for younger children, as they need rest periods or naps (no matter how much they argue the opposite!).

Plan for a balanced schedule, like you did using the one-day planning sheet earlier. As a final preparatory note, have everything you need purchased and in place ahead of time so you don't need to dart back and forth to the store every day.

For school-age children, try to include some chores and ongoing projects around the house, like clearing a patch of ground and planting a vegetable garden, or working in the wood shop to build a birdhouse. Children in grade school are especially suited for projects taken in stages. They will love learning to do the things that you enjoy as hobbies, and besides filling up the time, they will help them to get to know you, and the things that you enjoy.

## Number of Children

If you are having more than one grandchild visit at a time, you will enjoy it more if you can spend small amounts of time alone with each one of them. It isn't necessary to plan distinctly separate activities unless there is a major age difference. Many older children will join in with whatever you have in mind for their younger sibling, if only because it has been a long time since they have done the activity. Arts and crafts are especially helpful for entertaining multiple ages as the grandchildren can work side by side at their own projects and at their own pace.

## Meeting Basic Needs

Young children are generally early risers and voracious eaters who have little patience with waiting. There will be no doubt about when toddlers or preschoolers are hungry or tired. It will always be necessary to plan for meal stops, as well as to carry emergency eating provisions like crackers and cheese for unexpected delays in traffic or bank lines.

Expect that naps and bedtimes will be vigorously opposed by all young grandchildren and be prepared to plan for ways to "trick" the youngest ones into slowing down for an afternoon rest. A gentle back rub while listening to taped stories or soft music often works (as long as you don't fall asleep first!).

Teenagers can astound you with their surprising abilities to sleep, so don't be surprised, or offended, if your plans for a perfect day go awry when they sleep in late, or stretch out on the sofa all afternoon. Enjoy the fact that these are the same children who resisted sleep so vigorously just a few years ago!

As with the single-day visit, planning is everything. Begin by sketching out a plan for the whole week, using a planning sheet like the following one so that you have a framework to guide you through days of pleasant times together.

As a closing thought on visits, most of what has been said also applies to trips you make to visit your grandchildren at their homes. If you haven't seen your grandchildren for a while, you won't want to

*Rule 6:* GRANDPARENTS SHOULD BE FULL OF FUN IDEAS

**SAMPLE WEEKLY VISIT PLAN**

| | Morning | Afternoon | Evening |
|---|---|---|---|
| SUNDAY | help make breakfast, art, house chores | picnic by the river; pick blackberries, collect leaves, rocks for art tomorrow. | video, fresh berry pie |
| MONDAY | farmer's market, library | read books, rest, begin to clear garden, make collages from river collection | walk to get yogurt, fly kite, begin long adventure book |
| TUESDAY | work on garden, make lunch pizza | books and rest, tea party, wash doll clothes outside | park picnic, bubble bath, continue adventure book |
| WEDNESDAY | make dried fruit people, plant garden | lunch out, music tapes and rest, water play outside | help make dinner, bake cookies, bike ride, continue book |
| THURSDAY | breakfast picnic at park, water garden, make granola for tomorrow | tapes and rest, sewing buttons, make fruit salad for dinner | movie at theater |
| FRIDAY | eat granola, water garden, art | lunch by river, sewing, stories and rest | concert at park, bike ride |
| SATURDAY | water garden, pack picnic for zoo | Kids' Day at the zoo, picnic | barbecue, family games |

waste one precious moment once you get there. The best way to get reacquainted can prove to be the hardest, for it means giving grand-children control over the pace. Once trust is reestablished (a quick process if they are in charge) you will be on your way!

To win over toddlers or young children who don't know you well, resolve to sacrifice your immediate desire to hug and kiss and adjust to their pace.

Try sitting quietly in a chair, holding something interesting. Toddlers and preschoolers will be too curious to resist the urge to explore, and left to their own, they will be at your side in no time. Then you will be able to let loose with those saved-up hugs and kisses!

Mail grandchildren who are unfamiliar with you a recent picture of yourself before you arrive. Write a letter or make a phone call describing some of the things you would like to do with them when you visit. Add some anecdotal information about yourself when you were their ages. Let them see you for the friendly person that you are. It might make them feel a little less shy when you do arrive, adding precious time together as soon as possible.

# ANNUAL GET-TOGETHERS

As grandchildren get older, it is possible to have successful events with all of them at the same time. Some grandparents begin their own wonderful family traditions of annual trips when grandchildren are old enough to travel away from home.

For one glorious week, weekend, or night over, these grandparents have a chance to love, pamper, spoil, educate, and entertain their grandchildren as they head out and do something that they all love (or have learned to love). Some grandparents set up a separate savings account for this purpose, so that they have resources set aside to go to a special family resort, or other outdoor destination where the grand-children can learn to water-ski, fish, or boat.

As grandchildren get older, they can help to research and plan these annual outings so that they enjoy it even more! Vacation trips can build skills, values, and closeness with cousins.

Some organizational tips to help make this time together the best it can be could include:

- Make reservations well in advance so there are minimal disappointments.
- Make a list of what each grandchild likes to do and provide something in the schedule to meet those needs.
- Plan at least one activity that will be new and will build competency.
- This kind of outing can be done alone, but it will be easier with two adults.
- Plan the days carefully, just as you would if you were having grandchildren at your home.
- Set behavior rules ahead of time with the grandchildren and insist on compliance.

# ACTIVITIES TO GET YOU STARTED

It doesn't take a lot of money to have a good time. For one thing, you can capitalize on the natural creative abilities that each of your grandchildren have. Add your own special talents (yes, you have them!) and be sure to explore some kind of new activity together.

## Cooking

Beyond obvious survival purpose, there is a tremendous value in letting both granddaughters and grandsons experience the joys of cooking with you. Both sexes are expected to know their way around the kitchen today and doing it together will be even more fun!

Who would ever dream that scientific properties like mass, volume, weight, and measurement could be so much fun? You can lead your grandchildren through a discovery of where food comes from, how food reflects a diversity of world cultures, and how to follow the sequence of a recipe to produce a predictable end product.

You can model good nutrition through your recipe selections and you can also enhance your grandchildren's math, science, social studies, and language skills without your grandchildren even knowing it!

Two-year-old grandchildren can pour and mix, activities that may be new and quite exciting. As your grandchildren count eggs, or struggle to find words to describe the smells, appearances, and tastes they experience, they will be practicing valuable skills. For the older grandchild, cooking is the *only* way to learn fractions and measuring!

# Menu Planning

If grandchildren are coming for a meal, why not let them help make the menu choices and assist with the preparation? If they are staying for a few days, you can use a menu planner like the following one to let them plan their menus for the whole stay. Follow the planning session with a trip to the grocery store so they can help locate and price the necessary ingredients. You will all but eliminate any fuss about eating, and they will consider you to be a totally cool grandparent!

**SAMPLE LUNCH PLAN**

*Select a sandwich:*

| | |
|---|---|
| _____ apple and cheese | _____ turkey and apricot |
| _____ bacon, lettuce, tomato | _____ meat loaf |
| _____ egg salad | _____ bologna and cheese |
| _____ cheese, tomato, lettuce | _____ ham and cheese |
| _____ peanut butter and jelly | _____ chicken salad |
| _____ tuna salad | _____ other |

*Pick a fruit:*

| | |
|---|---|
| _____ apple | _____ applesauce |
| _____ apricot | _____ banana |
| _____ peach | _____ melon cubes |
| _____ orange | _____ pineapple |
| _____ nectarine | _____ pear |
| _____ other | |

*Choose a vegetable:*

| | |
|---|---|
| _____ broccoli | _____ carrot sticks |
| _____ celery sticks | _____ snow peas |
| _____ raw cauliflower | _____ cherry tomatoes |
| _____ cucumber slices | _____ other |

*Pick a beverage:*

_____ milk                          _____ fruit juice

_____ other

*Vote for a treat:*

_____ dried fruit roll              _____ fig bar

_____ granola bar                   _____ pretzels

_____ string cheese                 _____ sunflower seeds

_____ trail mix                     _____ yogurt

_____ rice cake                     _____ pudding

_____ other

## Selecting Recipes

There are many excellent children's cookbooks in libraries and book-stores, so why not buy one for your grandchildren, or take them shopping to pick out one of their own. Some example of particularly good ones include:

*The Mother Goose Cookbook: Rhymes and Recipes for the Very Young* by Marianna Mayer, William Morrow and Co., 1998. (Ages 4 to 8.)

*The Little House Cookbook: Frontier Foods from Laura Ingalls Wilder's Classic Stories* by Barbara Walker, Harper Trophy, 3rd edition, 1995. (Ages 9 to 12. Captures the true pioneer spirit based on the beloved *Little House* books.)

*Roald Dahl's Revolting Recipes* by Roald Dahl, Viking Children's Books, 1994. (A school-age favorite! Dishes that sound worse than they taste: Stink Bug Eggs, Fresh Mudburger, and more!)

Cooking offers a different kind of reading experience and it can stimulate the imagination, as the suggestions listed above show. Supplement new recipes with a few of your own favorite tried and true recipes and allow your grandchildren to do as much of the work as possible by themselves, under your watchful supervision. Two-year-olds can pour and stir while five-year-olds measure and crack eggs.

A few ideas are provided below to help illustrate age appropriateness in recipes where active participation and good nutrition are your goals.

## SNACKS

*Quick Cherry Pies*

**Ages 2+**
refrigerator biscuits
canned pie filling
butter
flour

Dust surface with flour and let the child roll a biscuit into a circle with a rolling pin. Place a spoonful of filling in the center and dot with butter. Fold over and bake at 350° until brown, about 7 to 10 minutes.

*Orange Jupiter*

**Ages 2+**
1 3/4 cups powdered milk
1 1/4 cups powdered orange drink mix
small pkg. vanilla pudding mix

Mix ingredients and store in an airtight container. To make a serving, blend 3 heaping tablespoons of mix with 1/2 cup water and 2 ice cubes in a blender.

*Apple Gelatin Blocks*

**Ages 3+**
2 envelopes unflavored gelatin
4 cups applesauce
1 tsp. cinnamon
2 small pkgs. apple or lemon gelatin

Sprinkle unflavored gelatin over applesauce. Add cinnamon and stir. Microwave on high for 4 to 5 minutes until bubbling. Add flavored gelatin and stir until it melts. Pour into an 8-inch dish and refrigerate several hours until firm. Cut into 1-inch squares.
  Also good with strawberries and strawberry gelatin.

*Crunchy Granola*

**Ages 4+**

2 cups rolled oats

1/2 cup wheat germ

1/2 cup brown sugar

1 cup finely chopped nuts

1/4 cup flour

1 tsp. cinnamon

1/2 cup raisins

1/2 cup dried fruit

1/2 cup cooking oil

3 tbs. water

Mix together the first eight ingredients. Drizzle oil and water over and mix well. Press into a 9x13 inch glass baking dish and cook in a microwave for 4 minutes on high. Press down and cook again 2 to 3 minutes longer. Let stand until cooled and store in an airtight container.

**BREAKFAST IDEAS**

*Baked Apple Slices*

**Ages 3+**

1 cooking apple

1 tbs. butter

1 tbs. brown sugar

Peel apple and let your grandchild slice it into pieces with a plastic knife. Place in a dish and sprinkle with brown sugar and dot with butter. Cook in microwave on high for 1 to 2 minutes until butter melts. Cover with plastic wrap and cook 2 to 3 minutes longer until apples are tender. Let cool before removing wrap!

*Applesauce Muffins*

**Ages 3+**

1/2 cup applesauce

1 large banana

1 cup raisins
3/4 cup apple juice
1/4 cup oil
1 egg
1 tsp. vanilla
1/4 tsp. salt
1 tsp. cinnamon
1/2 cup wheat flour
1 tsp. baking soda

Pour apple juice, applesauce, banana, egg, oil, and vanilla into a blender and blend about 1 minute until smooth. Combine remaining ingredients in another bowl and add blender mixture. Add raisins and stir well. Bake in greased muffin tins 25 to 30 minutes at 375°.

*Scrambled Eggcup*

**Ages 3+**
2 tsp. butter
1 egg
1 tbs. milk

Melt butter in a Styrofoam cup for 30 seconds in a microwave. Add egg and milk and stir well. Cook on high for 25 seconds. Stir. Return and cook 15 to 25 seconds longer. Remove while still wet and soft. Eggs will set if you let them stand a few seconds before serving.

**MAIN DISH IDEAS**

*Crazy-Topped Potato*

**Ages 2+**
baking potato
toppings (cheese, sour cream, butter, bacon bits, grated
    carrots, alfalfa sprouts, green peas, etc.)

Wash potato and pierce several times with a fork. Cook on high in a microwave for 5 minutes, or until soft (7–8 minutes for two potatoes). Wrap in a kitchen towel and let stand 5 minutes. Cut open and add toppings of choice.

*Chicken Baked in Foil*

**Ages 2+**

For each small serving:

1-inch piece of uncooked chicken

1 sliced mushroom

1-inch piece of sweet potato

1 tsp. grated cheese

butter

Butter a 6-inch square of foil and arrange ingredients, topping with the cheese. Fold and seal. Bake at 375° for 15 minutes.

*Vegetable Soup*

**Ages 3+**

1 pkg. dry soup mix

1 qt. boiling water

salt to taste

soup bones

1 cup sliced celery

1 cup sliced carrots

1 chopped onion

1 1/2 cups sliced cabbage

(other vegetables your grandchild likes)

1 8-oz. can tomato sauce

Softer vegetables can be cut with plastic knives. Simmer all ingredients except tomato sauce for 2 hours. Add sauce and simmer 1 hour more. The smell will bring them to the table!

# Drawing

Drawing is an activity that comes naturally to children. It is also an important developmental step in the evolution of the ability to write. Children throughout the world draw in much the same way, adding the same drawing techniques, in pretty much the same order.

Your grandchildren will delight in scribbling at an early age if they are shown how. By age two, attempts are made to place lines on the paper, and eventually intersecting lines and circles are added. The four-year-old combines all of this experience into a (somewhat) recognizable picture that contains a whole story if you let them tell you about it.

By age five, the child is quite good at drawing and will create pictures for you with great enthusiasm, emphasizing the things that they consider important. Thus, you will see large heads (the most important feature to the child) with arms and legs coming out of them. The trunk is added later, along with finishing touches like belly buttons and eyelashes at about age five, signaling a maturity in perception and a heightened readiness for reading.

From age five on, drawing begins to explore elements like design, color, and pattern, with an assortment of complex artwork appearing to delight your eyes. Detailed pictures, many three dimensional without any formal training in perspective, tell marvelous stories without words. If you want to know what your grandchildren are thinking, ask them about their creations.

It takes thousands of scribbles, designs, and drawings to develop the skills through which drawing evolves into writing.

You can help that process by giving those precious little fingers lots of practice and exercise with a wide variety of drawing materials. The suggestions below can help you to offer a full repertoire of interesting variations.

*Basic Drawing*

**Ages 2+, quiet, 1/2 hr.+**

crayons, regular or fat

chalk, wet or dry

felt tip markers

pencils

ballpoint pens

paper of all kinds: butcher, computer, bags, gift wrap

Keep lots of these supplies on hand and let your grandchildren know that they can use them whenever they want. If they don't live nearby, mail supplies to them and encourage them to mail pictures of their creations back to you.

*Life-Size Body Portraits*

**Ages 2+, moderate activity level, 1/2 to 2 hrs.**

roll of white butcher paper

felt pens

scissors

Roll out a sheet of paper slightly larger than the child. Have your grandchild lie down, face up. Trace around their body, including ponytails, cowlicks, shoelaces, pants, etc. Let them color in the features while you add names and dates. You can give older children scraps of fabric, yarn, and buttons to glue on for finishing touches. Make copies to staple together and stuff with newspaper, if desired.

*Crayon Rubbings*

**Ages 3 to teens, quiet, 1/2 hr.+**

white paper

peeled crayons

  (bits and pieces of old crayons are great!)

objects to rub: pine needles, coins, sandpaper, leaves, etc.

Put an object under the paper and rub the peeled crayon over the surface. Object will show through as a print. Take a walk to see what you can capture on paper together!

*Melted Crayons*

**Ages 3 to teens, quiet, 1/2 hr.+**

food warming tray

peeled pieces of crayons

paper

foil

sponge

Kids love this one, and the activity is safe when supervised. Place foil on the heating tray and heat to low heat. Place paper on the foil and move peeled crayons over the paper. The crayon will glide and melt easily onto the paper when the temperature is right, creating a beautiful stained glass effect!

## Crafts

Your home can become a treasure trove just by saving the odds and ends that you usually throw away. Let your grandchildren turn them into recycled creations. There are many skills for children to learn as they create treasures from used materials:

---

*Giant Milk Carton Blocks*

**Ages 18 mo. to 4 yrs., active level, 1/2 to 1 hr.**

half gallon milk cartons (as many as you can save)

self-sticking shelf paper

You make these for your youngest grandkids. Wash them out and cut off the pouring spout. Take two cartons and push them together, one inside of the other. Cover with decorative shelf paper, if desired.

*Feed the Birds*

**Ages 2 yrs.+, quiet**

cookie cutters

yarn

peanut butter

bread

birdseed

Make a special meal for the birds in your neighborhood using cookie cutters to cut shapes from stale bread. Spread peanut butter on the shapes, sprinkle with birdseed, and thread a piece of yarn through each shape and hang the bread outside on a tree near a window. It may take several days for the birds to find this new source of food, but when they do, you will be able to watch them enjoying their meal!

*Paper Plate Hats*

**Ages 2 to 5, moderate activity level, 1/2 to 1 hr.**

large and small paper plates

stapler or tape

ribbon or string

hole puncher

---

coloring and decorating materials

glue

Punch two holes and string ribbons through a small plate. This will fit on the child's head. Staple or tape a large plate to the small one and decorate it by coloring, gluing cotton balls, painting, etc.

## Colored Macaroni Jewelry

**Ages 4 to 8, quiet level, 1 hr.+**

raw salad macaroni

rubbing alcohol

food coloring

yarn

nail polish or glue

To color the macaroni, put it in a jar with a little alcohol and food coloring. Shake to coat. Spoon onto paper towels and let dry. Stiffen end of a piece of yarn by wrapping with tape or dipping in glue. Let grandchildren string into necklaces and bracelets. Variations: add pieces of cut plastic straws or cereal pieces with holes.

## Nail Designs

**Ages 3 to 6, active level, 1/2 to 1 hr.**

large-headed nails

hammer (small)

piece of smooth lumber about 1 foot square

Make designs with nails by hammering them into the wood in patterns. Colors and textures improve with rain and wind exposure, turning ungalvanized nails a rich bronze color.

## Life-Size Foil Figure

**Ages 3+, moderate level, 1/2 hr.**

roll of heavy-duty foil

scissors

tape

Cut two pieces of foil about 5 feet long. Tape sheets together. Child lies on the floor and poses while you mold the foil to their body, beginning at the feet. Lift carefully and trim off around the edges. Tack to the wall or hang from a string.

### Invisible Ink

**Ages 5+, quiet level, 1/2 hr.**
lemon juice
Q-tips
white paper

Grandchildren write secret messages using a Q-tip dipped in lemon juice on white paper. Messages can only be decoded by heating with a warm iron! Older children will love to do it themselves while you sit nearby.

### First Sewing

**Ages 4+, quiet, 1/2 to 1 hr.**
Styrofoam meat trays
thin yarn
large needle

Wash and dry meat trays. Thread a large needle with yarn, demonstrate, and then watch them go! For added interest when the basic concept is mastered, add small scraps of loose-knitted fabric to attach.

### Newspaper Building Dowels

**Ages 7+, moderate level, 1 hr.+**
newspapers
masking tape

Roll single sheets of newspaper into tight dowels, starting at one corner and rolling diagonally. Secure with tape. Connect dowels with additional tape and watch as creations take shape!

### Food Print Paper

**Ages 3+, moderate level, 1 hr.+**
fruit and vegetables

white butcher paper

tempera paint

Cut food pieces in half. Dip lightly in paint and print on paper. This can get messy, so be prepared to stop occasionally to clean up when things get too slippery.

*Handprint Paper*

**Ages 2 to teens, quiet level, 1/2 to 1 hr.**

white or solid colored paper

tempera paint

Put a small amount of paint in a shallow saucer. Dip hand in lightly, covering all fingers. Place on paper to make prints. Wash hands between colors. Variation: use feet.

*Shimmer and Shine Wrap*

**Ages 6 to teens, quiet level, 1 hr.+**

heavy duty aluminum foil

colored tissue paper

glossy acrylic polymer

　(available at art stores)

small paintbrushes

Cut tissue paper into small pieces. Mix some polymer with a little water and brush over tissue paper that has been arranged on the foil. (It will act like a glue.) Let dry thoroughly. Note: Watch closely to keep fingers out of eyes!

# Play Dough

Children experience great satisfaction from handling just about any kinds of dough, and there are few activities that can calm an agitated child better.

If you bake bread, you have a natural dough available and your grandchildren can eat the finished product when they are done. If you don't bake, there are lots of easy alternatives that work just as well. Try any of the recipes below and consider rolling up your sleeves and joining in the fun.

*Basic Play Dough*

**Ages 2 to 8, moderate level, 1/2 to 1 hr.**

1 cup flour

1/3 cup salt

1 tbs. cream of tartar

1 tbs. oil

1 cup water

Mix together all ingredients. Younger children like to mold with their hands. Older grandchildren will enjoy plastic knives, cookie cutters, spatulas, etc. For variety, use food coloring, flavor extracts (for the scent), or warm water. Store in sealed container.

*Peanut Butter Play Dough*

**Ages 4+, moderate level, 1/2 to 1 hr.**

1 cup peanut butter

1/4 cup honey

powdered milk

Mix peanut butter and honey. Sprinkle in powdered milk until desired consistency. Use like play dough, except that nibbling is permitted! Store in sealed container in the refrigerator.

Goop (My favorite!)

**Ages 2 to teens, moderate level, 1/2 to 1 hr.**

1/2 cup cornstarch

1/4 cup water

plastic tub

You will love this as much as your grandchildren! Mix ingredients in a plastic tub with the hands and watch what happens. For variety, add food color, scented flavorings, or warm water.

## Collage and Sculpture

The word *collage* comes from the French and means "to paste," which is exactly what your grandchildren can do with odds and ends that you have around your house, or the things that they collect on walks. Watch them create one-of-a-kind art pieces of surprising beauty!

Sculpture is another form of three-dimensional art that helps children learn geometric perspectives. Like drawing, it allows children to explore the concepts of perspective, balance, weight, space, form, and color.

*Basic Collage*

**Ages 2 to teens, quiet level, 1/2 hr.+**

small, light pieces of odds and ends

something to glue them on, such as Styrofoam trays,
    paper, cardboard

white glue

Make designs by gluing materials onto the chosen surface. Suggestions of things to glue on include buttons, scraps of wood, pinecone pieces, cloth, eyelets, leaves, pebbles, cut up old greeting cards, wrapping paper, wallpaper. Let the child organize how things should be glued on. Young children will tend to clump them together. Older grandchildren will make elaborate and purposeful designs.

*String Art*

**Ages 3+, quiet level, 1/2 to 1 hr.**

pieces of string, yarn

scissors

glue

heavy cardboard

finger bowl with water

Water down the glue slightly and place in a saucer. Dip yarn and string into the glue-water mixture. Dry slightly by running between the fingers and place on the cardboard to dry.

*Marshmallow Sculptures*

**Ages 3+, quiet level, 1 hr.**

toothpicks

frosting

marshmallows, large and small

Assemble mini-sculptures while enjoying some finger licking along the way! Allow to dry and harden. This is a good use for leftover frosting.

*Noodle Art*

**Ages 4+, quiet level**

noodles of all shapes and sizes

white glue

waxed paper

spray paint (optional)

Glue noodle pieces together into lacy designs so that pieces touch lightly. Let dry at least 2 hours. Spray paint for Christmas ornaments, if desired.

*Wood Scrap Forms*

**Ages 3+, quiet level, 1/2 to 1 hr.**

small wood scraps

empty thread spools

small twigs and branches

white glue

This activity needs no directions, just lots of raw materials, space, and a playful grandparent!

*Tinfoil Sculpture*

**Ages 5+, moderate level, 1/2 to 1 hr.**

tinfoil

small twigs

yarn

Using pinching and molding techniques, create lifelike renditions of foil folks and other glittering objects.

## Painting

Watching grandchildren work with paint provides clues about the importance of this activity. The body movements and facial expressions mirror the inner experience that is taking place. Sometimes, a flood of language will erupt spontaneously. Something very real is going on inside and it is fascinating to behold!

The easiest paints to keep on hand and to clean up are watercolors and temperas. Both are inexpensive and available at drug and art stores. They can be stored for a long time so they make a good investment even if the grandchildren visit infrequently. Red, yellow, white, and black are good beginning choices because your grandchildren will accidentally create new colors as they mix the primary ones.

*Creamy Finger Painting*

**8 mo.+, moderate activity level, 1 1/2 hr.+**

canned shaving cream,

canned whipped cream or pudding

This is finger painting at its best! Place a small amount of any of the above materials on a clean, smooth surface and watch the grandchildren go. Supervise young artists to make sure their fingers stay out of their eyes. Shaving cream artists clean your table as they work. Be sure to catch a snapshot of the action.

*Painting with Water*

**Ages 2 to 5, moderate to active level, 1/2 to 2 hrs.**

paintbrushes of all sizes

bucket of water

Try this one in the summer. Put on the swimsuits and let your grandchildren paint the world, including the sidewalks, house, and car. Pour a glass of lemonade for yourself and pull up a chair to relax.

*Ice Painting*

**Ages 2 to 4, moderate activity level, 1/2 hr.**

block of ice, frozen in an empty half gallon cardboard milk carton

1/2 inch paintbrushes

tempera paint in at least three colors

Remove the ice from the carton and place in a shallow baking pan. Set out brushes and paint and watch the magic begin!

*Color Jar*

**Ages 3 to 5, quiet, 1/2 hr.**

clear glass jar

food colorings

Outfit the grandchildren with aprons or old shirts. Fill the jar with water and let your grandchildren put in food coloring, a drop at a time. Do not shake. Observe color changes.

*Silly Painting*

**Ages 3+, quiet, 1/2 hr.**

painting tools like Q-tips, feathers, cotton balls

paper

water or tempera paints

Surprise your grandchildren with a nontraditional paintbrush and watch them get creative. For younger children, introduce one tool at a time and switch when they get bored.

*Food Color Painting*

**Ages 4+, quiet, 1/2 hr.+**

food coloring

paper towels or coffee filters

eye droppers (available at pharmacy)

Mix food coloring in little dishes with a few teaspoons of water. Drop each color from an eyedropper onto filters or paper towels and watch colors spread and blend. Hang by clothespins to dry.

*Under-the-Sea-Pictures*

**Ages 3+, quiet, 1 hr.**

white paper

crayons

thin blue tempera or watercolor

Let your grandchildren scribble and draw on white paper with crayons (sea creatures are nice). When they have finished, let them cover their drawings with blue paint.

## Mud, Sand, and Water Play

These basic play materials have been enjoyed by children for thousands of years and if you are willing to let your grandchildren get wet and dirty, you can create some very special memories while keeping them happy and busy.

Playing with mud, sand, and water is especially good for passing the time on long, hot summer afternoons. Swimsuits are the best attire for this play because you can hose them off when they are finished.

Water in a plastic basin or wading pool is a good way to begin, as long as you stay close by to enjoy the fun. For variety, let your grandchildren wash dolls and dishes in a tub of soapy water, or set them to digging tunnels in a plot of dirt, flooding it with a hose to make waterways and moats. The possibilities for fun are endless!

To add further challenge and interest, add any of the following props:

| | |
|---|---|
| soup ladles | bulb baster |
| slotted spoon | fishing bobbers |
| strainer | peanuts in the shell |
| measuring cups | medicine droppers |
| small pitchers | empty thread spools |
| cooking tongs | squeeze bottles |
| corks | aquarium nets |
| scoops | small wood scraps |
| Styrofoam | empty spice cans |
| meat trays | empty cardboard |
| Ping-Pong balls | milk cartons |
| lids | small soap bars |
| egg beater | food coloring |
| sugar shaker | foil balls |
| bottle brush | rubber gloves |
| dish detergent | margarine tubs |
| candy thermometer | dry pasta |

## Woodwork

Woodworking can be adapted to any age grandchild, beginning at about age four. At first, you will do most of the work, allowing grandchildren the last blow to the nail, or the final few strokes with the sandpaper.

Grandparents who do woodwork with their grandchildren will be remembered for the wonderful smell of sawdust, the exciting feel of sandpaper, and the screech of the electric drill. Some of the happiest memories can emerge from the wood shop. Birdhouses, robots, and racing cars are the products, but the side effects include learning safety with tools, competency with handling them, trust, creativity, and the ability to plan, execute, and finish a project.

When your grandchildren hold their own finished products, they will beam from ear to ear and you can be proud of their achievements, relishing the memories of how they created them.

## Exercise

As children approach the elementary school years, it becomes more and more socially important for them to master physical skills, including the use of balls and bats, hoops, rackets, and all of the things that go with them. A drive for excellence makes ball playing a natural activity and offers grandparents a chance to enjoy teaching the basics.

Even babies will like to sit on the floor and roll a ball back and forth. A toddler will love taking turns kicking one across the yard. By age four, a grandchild can graduate to T-ball, or a set of plastic golf clubs to hit balls across the yard. By age seven or eight, they can use real equipment and learn how to care for it.

If golf is a game you want to share, go to the miniature golf course to introduce your grandchildren to the game. A trip to a driving range could be the next step and by age ten they can probably do the front nine without overtiring.

You can teach your grandchildren to dribble a basketball and to shoot at a hoop, or swing a small tennis racket at tennis balls that you throw carefully in their direction. Sharing ball sports with your grandchildren can improve their skills so that they can become more physically competent, and can provide you with many happy hours as you watch them compete on teams, or when you take them out for a round of golf, or a set of tennis.

## Games

Games teach sportsmanship and cooperation as well as social and motor skills, but it takes time and experience to learn to play them well. You can help to develop a tradition of family game fun by being an enthusiastic participant. Round up the grandchildren after dinner and take them to the family room for a good game.

*Walking with a String*

**Ages 12 to 18 mo., moderate, 15 to 30 mins.**

old shoe string, or piece of thick yarn about 3 feet long

Take a string and give one end to your toddler grandchild while you hold the other. Take turns signaling each other about which way you are going to go as you take a walk.

*Follow the Leader*

**Ages 18 mo.+, active, 1/4 to 1/2 hr.**

Nothing is needed to play this game. Demonstrate that you are the leader until your grandchildren understand what you are doing. Be sure to laugh along the way! For older children, weigh your ability to keep up because they will get rambunctious!

*Balloon Toss*

**Ages 2+, active, 1/2 hr.**

old blanket

inflated balloons

Everyone holds the edge of a blanket on which an inflated balloon has been placed. Toss the balloon up and down together, being careful not to let it fall out. Add more balloons if you want to increase the challenge.

*Silly Bones*

**Ages 4 to 6, active, 1/4 hr.**

This will cheer up any preschooler. Leader gives out commands like, "Touch elbows." While maintaining that touch another command is given such as, "Touch belly buttons." Play continues until no more commands can be followed and everyone is laughing.

*Bear Hugs*

**Ages 1 to 2, moderate, a few minutes**

Hug your toddler's teddy bear and then hand it back. Encourage your grandbaby to do the same and pass it back. Hug it and return it again. Don't be surprised if they don't want to stop!

*Bed Bouncing*

**Ages 18 mo. to 2 yrs., active, 1/4 hr.**

Every child loves to jump on the bed, so why not make a game of it? This works well if the child is twenty pounds or less. Stand next to a bed, facing each other with your grandchild on the bed. Jump up and down together holding hands. After ten or fifteen jumps, fall on the bed together. Beware! Toddlers have endless energy for this game!

*Penny-in-a-Bucket*

**Ages 3 to 8, quiet, 1/2 hr.**

plastic bucket

water

quarter

pennies

Fill the bucket with about 8 inches of water and place a quarter in the bottom. Grandchildren take turns dropping pennies into the bucket in an effort to cover the quarter. If they run out of pennies before the quarter is covered, the water wins.

*Keys and Locks*

**Ages 4 to 6, quiet, 1/2 hr.**

assorted padlocks with keys

Close all of the locks and let your grandchild find the key that fits each lock. This is a great car game.

*Quick Change*

**Ages 5 to adults, moderate, 1/2 hr.+**

Put players in pairs and have them face each other and observe how the person is dressed, how the hair is combed, etc. Turn away and change something: untie a shoe, move a watch, change the hair, etc. Turn around and have everyone try to figure out what has changed.

# Reading

If you leave your grandchildren with nothing more than a love of books, you are making a notable and valuable contribution to their lives.

Trips to the library introduce grandchildren to the joy of reading and help them to appreciate libraries as fun places to spend time. Consider making this a regular outing if you live nearby. Be sure to bring along your card, or phone ahead to find out what identification is needed to get your grandchildren cards of their own.

Many libraries have weekend or evening story times for children that sometimes include puppet shows, jugglers and magicians, and imaginative play.

You might also want to begin building your grandchildren a library of books at your house. Each book can be chosen carefully so that when you read and share them, the enjoyment flows both ways.

To get older grandchildren interested, try reading next to each other. Read the first few chapters of a book aloud, talking about what you have learned. Then, hand it over, pour the lemonade, and pull out a good book of your own, prepared for excited interruptions.

Some day, you will be able to look back through the collection that you have built up over the years and find the first book a grandchild ever read to you. You will find the serial stories you read your grandchildren over their summer vacations, and the teenage romance your granddaughter poured over at fourteen. It is likely grandchildren will share the same favorites with their own children someday, thanks to your interest and good example.

One way to make reading a popular activity at your home is to set up a comfortable and secluded place for it. It can be nothing more than a well lit corner and some throw pillows, or it could be a sofa next to a garden window, with a low shelf for books.

Whatever you can create, let grandchildren know that it is for their reading pleasure and make it as comfortable and inviting as possible. Then, share it with them often!

# Family Trees

At some point during the school years, you will get a frantic call asking for information on your family history for a school assignment. Why not get a jump on things and be ready for them?

A family tree is a visual representation of the factual information about your family history. It provides a valuable starting point for discussions of family history and values, as well as an understanding of where they fit into the family.

Libraries and bookstores will have many resources on how to create family trees, although you will have to do your own research to list the names of your own ancestors. If a family Bible has been passed down, there could be some helpful entries. If not, why not buy one and fill it out, going back at least two generations. You can pass it on so your grandchildren can see their names placed lovingly in it.

# Writing

There are few good letter writers in the world today, thanks to the easy and relatively low cost of the telephone and E-mail. Still, there is no thrill like finding a personal letter tucked in among the monthly junk mail.

You can continue to encourage letter and note writing as an appreciated form of communication, even if your grandchildren live nearby. Give your grandchildren a stack of stamped postcards and ask them to jot you notes when they are excited or angry.

If your grandchildren are hooked up to the Internet, you might consider getting an inexpensive computer and modem that will make letter writing by E-mail a snap. You can send notes back and forth without the bother of envelopes and postage. An added incentive is the fact that there are no long-distance telephone charges involved receiving notes by E-mail.

Other possible benefits of E-mail include the ability to tap into libraries, to contact magazines, to write to legislators, to practice foreign languages, and far, far more.

# Saving Money

At first glance, getting your grandchildren to save money hardly seems like an activity, but on further examination, it should be easy to see that it is one of the greatest skills that you could possibly gift a grandchild with. Attitudes on money are learned early in life and you can play a key role in that area of knowledge.

You can help grandchildren learn how to manage money, rather than doing it for them. Discuss your own money values, explaining in broad, general terms how you make spending decisions, how you save, and how you invest. Many children hear only negative comments about money as they are growing up and it is important for them to see money as a subject that is enjoyable.

It is also important to have conversations about what money doesn't do; that money is simply a tool, not an end to happiness, in and of itself.

Including books about handling money in your grandchildren's library is one way to introduce concepts to grandchildren. Some good possibilities of books written for children, rather than for their parents, include:

> In a world of economic diversity, it is important for children to understand and believe that net worth does not equal self-worth.

*The Berenstain Bears' Trouble with Money Book,* by Sam Berenstain, Random House, 1998. (Ages 4 to 8)

*One Dollar: My First Book About Money,* by Lynette Long, Barron's Juveniles, 1998. (Ages 4 to 8)

*The Kid's Guide to Money: Earning It, Saving It, Spending It, Growing It, Sharing It,* by Steven Otfinoski, Scholastic Trade, 1996. (Ages 9 to 12)

One useful way to help children plan their finances is to guide them into creating a financial plan all their own using a *third-third-third* plan. One-third can be spent immediately on things they want, one-third goes into short-term savings for future purchases of bigger items, and one-third goes into long-term savings that can't be touched.

The age at which children should get onto this savings track is debated, much as the issue of allowances. By ages six or seven, children are capable of simple planning and decision making. For further ideas, consult one of the many good new books on helping children handle money.

## Investing

Investing is a pastime that is definitely not limited to adults. Grade school children are fully capable of learning how the stock market works if you take the time to explain the basic goal of investing to them; to buy low and sell high. Books (simple beginner introductions to the stock market), the Internet, and materials provided by your broker, if you have one, can all help you to illustrate these basics.

You can help them find stocks that they are interested in, which will usually mean choices like McDonald's, Coca Cola, the Gap, and Disney. By making sure it is a product they understand and can identify with, the abstract concepts become more tangible.

A child cannot own stock directly, so you need a broker who can execute your grandchild's buy and sell orders, or you can open a custodial account listing both of your names. You can also use a discount broker or look for stocks that trade directly on the Internet. Some brokers will provide a break on commissions for your grandchildren's trades as a courtesy to you.

# Music

If music is a valuable part of your life, you will probably want it to be a part of your grandchildren's lives, too. Exposure to music can take many forms: music around your house, attendance at live performances, or offering to pay for instruments or music lessons for grandchildren who are interested in performing.

Scientists at the University of California at Irvine are confirming what music teachers have long suspected; music touches more than the soul, it touches the mind. Music exercises the whole brain and strengthens synapses in all brain systems. In other words, it actually increases the brain's capacity because it increases the strength of connections among the neurons.

The human voice is the cheapest musical instrument available, so ignore past doubts about whether you can sing and belt one out with your grandchildren, for they will love it! Records and tapes will always be appreciated. You don't need to buy a huge assortment of them, as youngsters prefer to sing and play their same favorites again and again.

# Relaxing

Spending time with grandchildren requires balance. It is fun to be on the move, but you can't keep going all of the time. A wise grandparent will help grandchildren learn how to create and enjoy quiet and relaxation.

One way to slow grandchildren down is to make slowing down so much fun that they don't want to resist it. Instead of demanding that they lie down and rest, lie down and do it with them, rubbing their backs and spoiling them with your love and attention. Invite them to stretch out on the bed with you, on a blanket in the yard, or at a park where you can tell each other stories while looking up at the clouds.

Teach them simple meditations by closing the eyes and focusing on breathing, measuring it in soft rhythms until you are both breathing quietly together. Soft music can help to set the tempo. Try stretching out on a mound of pillows to read a story that they love (preferably one without a lot of action!). Play some quiet music and give them a slow finger massage.

As you find what works with each grandchild, tailor relaxation methods to them and their individual abilities to remain quiet. You will be helping them to enjoy the good feelings that result, and the even better feelings when they get going again, renewed and refreshed! (Many adults would give anything to master this precious ability.)

# PLACES TO GO

Creating memories with your grandchildren also means taking them to places where you can have good times together. In the diapers and nap stages, outings need to be limited to short periods. Once grandchildren get older, the possibilities are endless.

There are more places to go than there is time to get there. You don't need to spend a fortune to enjoy your time together, but careful preplanning for all outings is essential and no outing with grandchildren, even a spur of the moment one, should be undertaken without basic considerations.

A good time together means that there are plans in place to meet the needs for toileting, eating, water, and weather conditions so that everyone can remain comfortable. Some suggestions are listed below to get your mind moving out and beyond the front doorstep. Discover the many new things that there are to do and explore together. The suggestions listed are rated by cost, as follows:

| | |
|---|---|
| $ | free or low cost |
| $$ | moderate cost |
| $$$ | costly |

You have waited for these wonderful days, so pack things up and get out there to make yourself some memories!

## Camping $

If this is an activity that you enjoy, why not share it with your grandchildren once they are old enough to be away from home? A few grandchildren at a time works best, unless you have compatible cousins or siblings who are used to being together.

Be sure to include your grandchildren in the campsite chores so that they can discover how much fun it is to work together to create a memorable camping experience.

## Playgrounds $

Children love to go to the playground where they can run and giggle and show off for you. Even teenagers like to fly high and free on a swing after a picnic lunch or dinner.

An important consideration in choosing a playground is if the equipment is safe. The National Program for Playground Safety notes that each year over 200,000 preschool and school-age children are injured on America's playgrounds. Although many cities and park districts across the country are pulling out old equipment and installing safer plastic playground equipment, some are still struggling with tight budgets to accomplish that end.

The safety group cites falls from slides and climbing equipment as the main cause of injuries for children up to age four. For children five and over climbing equipment is the main culprit. In all fairness, the frequency of falls at playgrounds is only slightly greater than falls on backyard play equipment and you will also need to weigh in your grandchildren's personalities as risk takers.

One of the best way to guard against injurious falls is to check the ground surface below equipment to be sure it is deep enough to absorb the shock of a fall. This requires at least nine to twelve inches of bark, sand, or one of the new rubber padded surfaces.

Many slides are up to sixteen feet tall and less than two feet wide. The platform at the top can lack adequate room for small children to get seated before the ride down. There should be protective siding, or a lip, to protect young children while they are performing this delicate maneuver.

Swings are a timely and beloved piece of equipment, as long as grandchildren don't walk into the path of a moving one. Merry-go-rounds (the metal kind that get pushed around in a circle) have definitely outlived their usefulness. They are usually either too close to the dirt or too high off the ground, making it possible to get trapped underneath.

If you are concerned that the playground in your neighborhood isn't safe, don't hesitate to contact the responsible party and let them know. If you still have doubts, you can go to one of the commercial playgrounds at fast-food outlets. They are not as aesthetically pleasing, but they are designed for safe play, and children love them.

## Nature Walks $

Taking a walk along the beach, a lake, or in the mountains will awaken your grandchildren's natural curiosity and might even reignite yours!

Bring along a bag lunch and a bag for collecting the marvelous little things that youngsters can never pass up. For preschoolers, you might issue challenges like finding items that are soft, bumpy, cold, green, etc.

## Picnics $

Rare is the grandchild who won't jump at the chance for a picnic, and one that Grandma and Grandpa put together is the best picnic of all! What fun to eat finger foods out of a bag, sharing them with cheerful company!

The setting doesn't need to be exotic or distant, although it is nice to get away from the home territory sometimes. On the spur of the moment, try the back lawn, a local park, the side of a country road, or the grass in front of the city library.

## Local Special Events $

Local newspapers are full of suggestions for special events in your community, many of them designed specifically for families. You can find seasonal, multicultural, and patriotic events, along with parades, festivals, and art shows. Mark seasonal events on your calendar and you will have a reminder to return to them next year.

## Park District Classes $

Many park districts offer reasonably priced recreation classes for preschoolers and school-age children, especially during holidays and summer. These interesting additions can help to fill time meaningfully during extended visits.

Crafts, nature programs, dance lessons, cooking classes, puppet shows, and holiday crafts are just some of the possibilities. Finish up with a picnic and jaunt to the adjacent playground and you will have some very happy grandchildren.

## Exploring Transportation $

Have your grandchildren ever taken a ride on a bus? That outing might sound boring to you, but young children have a fascination with buses and many have only seen them from a distance. Or, how about a ferry ride, or a trip on the light rail train?

Be sure to check on fares ahead of time in case you need correct change, and avoid transfers with small grandchildren who are not good at waiting.

## Art Galleries $

If you think that your grandchildren are too young for an art gallery, you could be in for a wonderful surprise. In limited doses, art galleries can spark children's natural curiosity and will make popular outings. As long as you are enthusiastic, your grandchildren will take their cues from you.

Tour just a room or two and then take a soda break and challenge grandchildren to tell you which pieces they like best, and why. Children who hate art galleries have usually been made to stay or to keep quiet too long. Check to see if the gallery has a children's room where kids are allowed and encouraged to touch the art.

## Historical Sites $

Contact local historical associations for ideas for interesting outings, taking into account the ages of your grandchildren. Many historical museums have displays geared to the interests of youngsters. Occasional outings of this type can enrich your grandchildren's view of the world and can prove helpful with their school lessons.

If there is an annual historical reenactment (Civil War, pioneer, living history) your children can experience history the fun way. If there is a picnic site nearby, you have a well-rounded day planned.

## Farms $

If you don't live on a farm or near an orchard, your grandchildren may love to spend a day exploring one. Many children have not seen fruit growing on trees, let alone had the chance to pick it.

Prices are generally good at orchards where public picking is allowed and you can go home after a fun day to bake a fresh fruit dessert that everyone will enjoy, knowing the part they played in its creation!

## Farmer's Markets $

Open-air markets are enjoying renewed popularity across the nation and they can be found in parks and urban malls everywhere. Children get a chance to see produce without plastic wrappings, most of it is pesticide free. Music, street entertainers, and food vendors round things off to make for a festive outing. Be sure to bring something home that your grandchildren can help you cook for dinner.

## Manufacturing Sites $

Contact local factories and find out if they offer public tours. Your grandchildren will be thrilled to see how chocolate bars, newspapers, or ice cream are made. A post office tour offers a fascinating look at how thousands of letters are moved on their way for delivery each day.

## Movie Theaters $$

For children used to home videos, a trip to a movie house can be a special treat. Choose the movie carefully and you won't have any unpleasant surprises. Asking children what they want to see is not always the best approach, because their suggestions are likely to be influenced by what is advertised on television.

To make your grandchildren feel that they have some say in the choice, you might let them select a movie from your two or three appropriate suggestions that you make. Matinees are good price wise, but the cost of treats are not generally reduced.

## Water Slides $$

Water slide parks are found throughout the country and are as popular with most older children as amusement parks. They are basically for children over age five who meet specific height requirements. Needless to say, teenagers will approve wholeheartedly of this choice.

The cost is a little high, but if there is a good shady spot nearby, you can settle into a lawn chair and enjoy a pleasant day. Bring along a good book and a hearty snack, for you will be reminded how hungry children get from water play.

## Amusement Parks $$$

If your grandchildren are older and there is an amusement park nearby, they have probably begged you to take them there already. Consider their request realistically as it could entail a fair amount of walking, heat, noise, and crowded lines. Thrill type rides are unsuitable for preschoolers, but for older children, they offer endless fascination. This makes a great outing to celebrate the beginning or end of the summer vacation.

## Trips with Grandchildren $$$

An intergenerational trip with grandchildren can be the highlight of your grandparenting years. If it is something that interests you, make sure that you do it in ways that work well for both the grandchildren and for yourself.

The key to traveling with grandchildren is to remember that you are not doing this *for* the grandchildren, you are doing this *with* them! That means that everyone needs to have a good time, to be as comfortable as possible, and to have their basic needs met along the way.

Trips can be for as short a time period as a weekend, for a few weeks, or for the whole summer, depending on what you want to see and how much money you have to spend. Planning should be spread out over the months before so that everyone can share in the decision making (understanding that you are making the final decisions!).

By planning for the following areas you can feel fairly confident that things will go smoothly.

## Cost

This is the first consideration if you will be paying all or part of trips. The idea is probably to offer your grandchildren something they couldn't afford to do on their own. Be very clear about what you will cover (put it into writing) and have grandchildren draw up their own budgets for spending money they will bring along for extras like souvenirs, film, and gifts.

## Destination

A trip to Europe would certainly be a lifetime highlight, but there is no need to go abroad to have a good time. There are many exciting places to visit right here in the United States. If you don't have a particular destination in mind, make a list of places that you would like to go and ask your grandchildren which interest them.

If it will be a lengthy trip, enlist the services of a good travel agent and get lots of informational brochures and maps so you can plan the route thoughtfully and realistically. You'll want to move fast enough to see everything, but not so fast that everyone gets exhausted.

The destination should have something for everyone, considering such things as amusement and theme parks, pools, spas and shopping, historical sights for learning value, and a change of landscape that demonstrates geographical diversity.

## Length of Trip

The length of the trip should be geared to how much money you want to spend and to the ages of the grandchildren you are taking along. Ages seven or eight are probably absolute minimums if the parents aren't coming along. Problems associated with being together so much can be mitigated by building in rest breaks and short periods of time away from each other.

## Transportation Mode

A mode that is new to your grandchildren will make your trip even more interesting to grandchildren. Trains, an occasional tour bus, and an airplane trip will all prove memorable.

Another possibility is a recreational vehicle (RV) trip. Rental vehicles come complete with bathrooms, tables, refrigerators, and plenty of room to stretch, so that you can easily meet the needs of everyone present. Campground fees are far less than motel room fees, and many family campgrounds have laundry facilities, showers, pools, spas, and friendly neighbors!

An alternate might be to take a cruise. Not only would the mode of transportation and the layout of the ship be exciting and new, but activities would be provided and planned for grandchildren of all ages. With the staff helping to watch the kids, you could easily build in the relaxation that you need to enjoy yourself.

## EXPLORING RULE 6 CONCEPTS

*Work through the issues below to help renew your skills in enjoying and playing with grandchildren.*

### 1. Does being in charge of grandchildren make me feel apprehensive?

*Always:*
• Say so and stick to visits and outings when the parents come.

*Sometimes:*
• Try having just one grandchild at a time with you.
• Limit the length of your time alone together.
• Make a list of things you enjoyed at their age and become that child again as you do them with grandchildren.
• If at first you don't succeed . . . (you know the rest!).

*Never:*
• You understand the meaning of the word *balance*.

### 2. Am I committed to creating good memories when grandchildren are with me?

*Always:*
• With that as a goal, fun can't help but happen!

*Sometimes:*
- Refocus on this goal if either of you becomes irritable or bored.
- At the end of a visit, ask grandchildren what they enjoyed the most and keep a running list.
- Take a photograph each time you are together and display them in one place.
- Extend the time together with a fun pack for on the way home (bag with small toys, crackers, stickers, crayons).

*Never:*
- Your favor is a favor to no one.

## 3. Do I consider myself to be a playful person?

*Always:*
- And your belief is probably a reality!

*Sometimes:*
- If you aren't having fun, try to identify what is getting in the way (unrelated problems, a health concern, something someone said to you).
- Watch a grandchild for half an hour. Jot down whenever they are *not* playful. How much fun is it to be around them during those times?
- Play the giggling game. Lay on the floor with your grandchild's head on your stomach and both of you try not to laugh.

*Never:*
- Commit to change and let your grandchildren teach you how. (Just do what they do!)

## 4. Do I allow grandchildren to do everything for themselves that they can?

*Always:*
- And they are proud of the results!

*Sometimes:*
- Remember that the more they do themselves, the more grown-up and competent they feel.
- Doing things for children can make them feel that you don't trust them, rather than that you love them.
- Get in the habit of saying, "Would you like to try . . ."
- Does it really matter if the food has a unique look, or if the silverware is in the wrong places?

130

*Never:*
- No wonder you feel exhausted after watching grandchildren!
- Have you noticed a lot of whining? It is their way of begging for more of what you are giving to them.

## 5. Have I given careful thought to grandchildren's play space at my home?

*Always:*
- You show them that they belong there.
- Their space has a full selection of art supplies that they can use whenever they want.
- They have their own library at your home.

*Sometimes:*
- It works, but it could be better.
- Resolve to clean out a space for this purpose.
- Plan a time when you can do it.
- Do it!

*Never:*
- No wonder the place is a mess after they go home!

## 6. Do I save odds and ends and plan exciting projects with them?

*Always:*
- Nothing gets thrown away anymore (egg cartons, meat trays, jars and lids, milk bottle tops, plastic bread sealers)!
- You are starting to see the world in a "recycled" way!

*Sometimes:*
- You do it when you remember.
- You have a system in place for collecting and storing materials.
- You ask friends to save things.

*Never:*
- You could be missing out on treasures left uncreated and laughter left unheard.

## Rule 7:
# GRANDPARENTS SHOULD LOVE ALL OF THEIR GRANDCHILDREN THE SAME

## **S**ECRETS OF THE HEART

Each and every grandchild is special. Each and every grandchild is welcomed with love and joy. Each and every grandchild deserves an equal share of love and attention . . . possibly.

Possibly? Isn't it understood that grandparents need to hold up the highest possible standard of love when it comes to their grandchildren; that they should share their bountiful love equally with them all? Doesn't it seem logical that grandparents should dispense love equally so that grandchildren will experience the true meaning of justice and fairness?

Unfortunately, when grandparents strive to love each grandchild with absolute equality, the results can be bland and mediocre. It is entirely possible that loving equally is the easy way out.

Perhaps the rule needs to say that grandparents should love all of their grandchildren intensely, and leave it at that! Trying to love each grandchild the same is a goal that can cause guilt and confusion, in large part because it is not necessarily a goal humanly possible to achieve! By nature, we have preferences, tastes, and inclinations, so why shouldn't there be specialized feelings for grandchildren who come with an individual shape, personality, and size?

The freedom to act as an effective grandparent can only come when the standard of equality is thrown out and the focus is put on loving each

132

grandchild uniquely and completely for who they are. To focus on intense feelings of love and appreciation for each individual grandchild is to celebrate the gifts that each of them brings into the world!

When it comes to dictating a system of strict fairness, grandparents can spend most (if not all) of their time doing just that, and they can be worn out at the end of it! It probably makes sense to cut the cake exactly in half to avoid a fight, but it is questionable whether it is desirable to cut time into neat, equal pieces, as if each grandchild requires exactly the same response from you. Each grandchild is a unique individual. Treating them according to their needs reinforces that important fact. Attention given to grandchildren is most effective when it is tailored to meet the needs of each particular child, and when it reinforces their particular needs for current growth and development.

To be an effective grandparent, it is necessary to go beyond the seeming simplicity of this rule and to strike out into some very personal and uncharted territory. It takes more time to seek out individuality than it does to mete out equality, but the rewards are far, far greater!

> Although frequently accepted at face value, the equal-love rule can undermine the very essence of grandparenting, which is to nurture each grandchild's uniqueness as only a grandparent can.

How can grandparents acknowledge differences in their feelings for grandchildren without being accused of playing favorites? Some ignore the challenge and serve themselves a hefty dose of guilt, striving to snuff out such feelings. Others accept their natural inclinations as tools to further the growth of each grandchild. They give each child what that child needs, knowing that by doing so they are playing favorites with each one of them!

There is nothing wrong with grandparents admitting that a grandchild appeals more readily at one time or another. Perhaps a grandchild shares more of their own personality traits, or enjoys more of the same things that they do. A grandchild might be at a more enjoyable developmental stage, or might have a personality that makes him or her easier to take places. In some cases, a grandchild who is difficult in some way (a fussy eater, light sleeper, etc.) becomes a favorite just because he or she needs more love and support.

When individual feelings for a grandchild arise, it isn't a question of loving that grandchild more. It is a question of reacting to each child for who they are, responding in differing ways, and enjoying the marvelous bonding and growth that result!

# HOW EQUAL DOES EQUAL NEED TO BE?

There is nothing wrong with grandparents admitting to themselves that natural differences in their feelings exist, as long as they don't treat any grandchild to less love.

> The question is not whether grandparents need to love their grandchildren equally, so much as whether they need to treat them with equal care and respect.

Treating grandchildren the same doesn't mean cutting the cake into six exactly equal pieces, or dividing a bag of candy into piles that contain the exact same number of green, red, and yellow pieces. Equal treatment means striving to give each child the love and attention that they need in order to grow and learn from contact with grandparents. It also means avoiding blatant favoritism by trying to make similar offers of love and attention, over the long run.

A grandchild trying to master a new skill, or one that is facing a problem can (and should) be given extra attention without having to feel that something is owed to other grandchildren. By making each child feel special, a grandparent will never have to worry about complaints of disparate treatment because each grandchild will be satisfied, knowing that the grandparent's love is constant and sustaining.

If you have more than one grandchild, it can be rewarding to keep separate journals with individual notes that include places each grandchild enjoys going, or activities and foods that they especially love. Taking the time to make notes can help to nourish a focus on each grandchild's individuality and it provides a larger view of your role in providing support and continuity.

Looking at grandchildren as the wonderful individuals that they are is easier if you have frequent access to them. If this is not the case, keeping a journal can be even more helpful. Occasional reviews of the information contained can help you to zero in on areas that you still need to explore.

Knowing as much about a grandchild as possible, including likes and dislikes, enables a grandparent to give what is needed. Test your knowledge of such detailed information by jotting down some of each grandchild's notable personality traits, along with a few concrete adjectives to describe what makes them special to you.

For example, you could note that your five-year-old grandson is easygoing, independent, headstrong, or talkative. Your granddaughter's entry might include a list of some of her favorite activities, foods, and toys. You could also benefit from listing some of the most memorable places and times you have spent together with each grandchild in the last few years; those times when you felt really close and connected.

# SIBLINGS

It is especially nice to have one grandchild at a time with you, but that isn't always possible. When more than one grandchild visits, a certain level of competition is to be expected. Even that can be minimized by meeting each child's needs on an individual, rather than on a competitive basis. Fighting and acting out with siblings and cousins is sometimes aimed at getting adult attention rather than settling conflicts, and giving individual attention to each child is the best way to cut down on such competitive, and attention-getting behavior.

If you choose play materials carefully so each grandchild knows you have their unique interests in mind and that you care about what they are doing, your gifts will be even more significant to them. And if you have enough of everything on hand so that sharing can be kept to a minimum, or if you rotate activities so everyone knows they will get a turn, you can eliminate much of the normal fighting and conflict.

Equal love, with individual treatment allows you to stop spending precious time dispensing justice instead of exploring just what that love means.

# STEP- AND ADOPTED GRANDCHILDREN

Grandparents are sometimes blessed with grandchildren in ways other than through biological birth. Divorce with remarriage and adoption can bring new grandchildren as well as grandchildren who are older and for whom there is no previous acquaintance.

## Step-Grandchildren
Today, many parents remarry during the course of raising their children, bringing grandparents new grandchildren. Some of these grandchildren

come with the new spouse, while others are the result of the new marital union. Grandparents can play a very central role in blended and stepfamilies. They can provide a source of love and affection, knowledge and humor, and a place where every child feels accepted for who they are.

Issues faced by blended families are many and complex, but for grandparents they provide an excellent opportunity to test this rule to the limit! How grandparents react to new grandchildren can play a key role in helping the transitions to go smoother for everyone involved.

In the beginning, grandparents can feel uncomfortable as they try to become acquainted with new grandchildren. Grandparents who have considered this rule seriously can make adaptations more easily because they will focus on the individuality and personality traits of new grandchildren, celebrating their uniqueness instead of lumping them together with their current grandchildren.

By learning their likes and dislikes, grandparents can integrate them more easily into family get-togethers and holidays. Gift giving is automatically equal when grandparents select gifts that are based on a growing knowledge of their interests. The only exception to equal treatment might be in the way the grandparent expresses affection. Biological grandchildren should not have to give up hugs and kisses just because grandparents don't feel comfortable kissing step-grandchildren.

Because of the focus on individuality, grandparents can test the waters and give new grandchildren a pleasant hug or light kiss when they seem ready. Reading their body language and adjusting accordingly will send new grandchildren messages of acceptance.

There are many practical ways for grandparents to help new marriages and blended families to succeed. The following suggestions provide some good ways to get started, letting nature take its course as friendships begin to take hold, and ideas flow on their own:

Volunteer occasional time baby-sitting so that the parents
 can be alone.
Begin a new family scrapbook that shows emerging traditions.
Modify family holidays in ways that will make everyone feel
 welcomed and included.
Avoid urges to criticize or judge.
Model acceptance of the new spouse in front of the grandchildren,
 but try to maintain a friendship with the former spouse, if possible.
Include step-grandchildren in routines like chores and cleanup.

Continue to have special times with your own natural grandchildren. Focus on the successes of all your grandchildren, old and new.

The equal love rule, where step-grandchildren are concerned, can be an unrealistic one if it makes demands that are humanly impossible. Grandparents needn't be too hard on themselves if the feelings of love don't come quickly, or at all. Their adult child fell in love and remarried, and that choice can take time to work through. Love grows over time, not on demand.

When you have known a grandchild since birth, it is easy to anticipate behaviors and reactions. With step-grandchildren the background is missing so that enforcing rules can feel awkward and uncomfortable. Fortunately, most children won't resist rules that are fair and that are explained in a calm manner, with ample allowance for dialogue.

Children in blended families are faced with demands to be extremely flexible and with admitting a widening circle of adults and children into their lives. There can be step-siblings with whom they have to share attention, belongings, and even living space. That is not an easy transition, even in the best of situations. There can be jealousy and confusion as blended families struggle to define how things are going to look when things settle into place. A grandparent's primary role is to continue to give love and attention exactly as they have all along, making themselves available to talk when they are approached.

If grandparents listen and pay attention, their grandchildren and step-grandchildren will show them what they need in order to ease into the changes. If grandparents have worked to be close, their grandchildren will feel comfortable unloading any of the confusing or negative feelings they are experiencing, safe in the knowledge that they won't be judged.

Grandparents are living proof that change is what life is about and that confusion can give way to times of understanding and renewed balance.

## Adopted Grandchildren

Adoption can also cause grandparents ambivalent feelings because of the extraordinary and unusual commitments that it entails. In reality, adoption proves that a grandparent has raised their child well, for the child is able to love enough to adopt. What a marvelous reflection on the grandparent!

In spite of the strong positive statement that adoption makes, ambivalent feelings can remain, causing grandparents to anguish over whether or not they will *feel* the same about adopted grandchildren.

There can be the added fear of vulnerability about giving love uncon-ditionally in case something goes wrong with the placement at a later date, or if the child has unforeseen medical or genetic problems.

A major transition like adoption can be easier if the child is young, for a baby of one or two months will take less time to adjust to its new family than a baby of eight months. By age three or four, adjustment can take even longer, depending on what has happened prior to the placement.

Grandparents can play a supportive role by demonstrating patience and understanding with the new child, whatever its age, as well as with the parents, who are beginning a rewarding new relationship of their own.

# A GRANDCHILD WITH A DISABILITY

Suspecting that a grandchild's development might not be normal is one of a grandparent's greatest fears. The term *disabled* can conjure up frightening mental pictures, many of them unfounded exaggerations of the truth. It is difficult for any grandparent to imagine how they would deal with a developmental abnormality, or what role they would play in the life of a disabled grandchild.

Disabilities encompass a wide range of physical and mental irreg-ularities. Some are hidden from view, while others are easy to detect. Some require minor family adjustments and others pose serious life-long implications.

Facing the possibility that something might be wrong with a grand-child can cause extreme apprehension and, in some cases, outright denial. The grandparents, like the parents, must come to grips with the realities of the situation before they can help the child begin to acquire the best coping patterns and skills possible.

Facing the situation becomes easier when more is learned about the particular disability from a medical and educational viewpoint. Ample resources are available to learn about disabilities including physicians, libraries, community organizations, the Internet, and bookstores.

It is not uncommon for the parents to be in denial, even as the clues mount up, so that grandparents often play the key role in speaking the unspeakable. With many disabilities, time is critical in providing appro-priate intervention and therapy, particularly in the case of young children or preschoolers. If it becomes obvious that a grandparent needs to speak up, he or she should probably be prepared for rebuttals, and even anger.

Grandparents who live nearby can help by accompanying the parent to diagnostic appointments, or by being available to watch siblings while they do so. They can be a sounding board for fears and frustrations, not an easy role to play, but certainly a very helpful one. It is important to focus on the fact that there can be no progress if the problem is ignored.

All children, even those with disabilities, sense how adults feel about them so that it is important for grandparents to continue to send them constant messages of love. If a disabled grandchild could share a few words of wisdom, he or she would probably include some of the following statements:

> Love me for who I am, not for who you would like me to be.
> Be my friend and help me like a friend would.
> Talk to me slowly like I am a person, not a baby.
> Give me time to do my best.
> Don't feel sorry for me.
> If I mess up, be patient and help me understand what I did wrong.

Learning disabilities are caused by difficulties with the nervous system that affect the receiving, processing, or communication of information. Most learning disabilities can be remedied through special education, therapy intervention, and assistive devices like hearing aids and glasses.

Learning disabilities can make it difficult for a child to concentrate, to follow instructions, or to behave at home or at school. When children cannot master tasks like their peers do, they can become understandably angry and frustrated.

Perhaps the most distressing period for everyone in the family to get through is the diagnostic phase. The local school district is one of the first places to contact, even for preschoolers. Schools can make referrals to other available services, even for infants. The child's pediatrician can make other appropriate medical referrals for additional screenings and tests. Family counseling can also be helpful for the family as they learn to cope with the realities of living with the disability.

Some signs of learning disabilities can include the following, usually in combinations with each other:

> extreme delays in motor or language skills
> difficulty understanding and following directions
> trouble remembering what someone has just said
> failure to master reading, writing, and math skills
>   at the expected age

confusing numbers and letters, such as mixing up
   twenty-five and fifty-two
extreme lack of coordination
frequent loss of items
difficulty understanding the concept of time

# SHARING WITH THE "OTHER" GRANDPARENTS

Grandchildren can have two sets of grandparents, and maybe even more if there has been a remarriage. Other sets of grandparents can make grandparents feel threatened, but fortunately this presents no problem where children are concerned. They come equipped with an unlimited capacity to love!

Any caring adult who wishes to have a loving relationship with a child can do so successfully. Children do not compare people for what they give, but rather for how they express love and caring. Best of all, any and all love that your grandchildren receive strengthens their emotional health and well-being.

> Your unique and special style of grandparenting is a reflection of your own set of personal values and beliefs and will be recognized as such by your grandchildren.

As they form relationships with other relatives, including grandparents, those relationships will differ from yours and they will be comfortable with those differences. They may delight in one grandfather's love of animals and gardening, and another grandparent's easy manner and ability to tell funny jokes. Likewise, one grandmother may be cherished for her never-empty cookie jar, and another for her marvelous adventure stories.

Creating grandparent memories is a personal challenge, not a competitive one. If the other grandparents have greater financial resources and can buy more things, that doesn't mean that they will automatically be better loved. Giving gifts doesn't lend an advantage, in and of itself. What children respond best to is genuine love and caring.

Your grandchildren's ability to love many people is a blessing that you can wholeheartedly encourage, safe in the knowledge that they won't measure and mete out love from a limited supply. If your grandchildren feel comfortable enough to tell you how they spend their time with the other grandparents, you should feel flattered. It is a compliment to you that they want to share their excitement with you and that they are secure in the knowledge that their position in your life is always solid.

# Exploring Rule 7 Concepts

*The following questions can help you to see how fortunate you are to have each grandchild as a part of your life!*

### 1. Do special qualities come to mind when I think about each grandchild?

*Always:*
- You can also name their favorite activities!

*Sometimes:*
- Perhaps you are trying too hard to be fair.
- It is more likely to happen when you have one grandchild at a time and you can focus on him or her.
- Tell each grandchild what you think is special about them in front of the family.

*Never:*
- You have become a scale of justice. Try to let things take a more natural course.

### 2. Do I make efforts to show each grandchild individualized love?

*Always:*
- You know everything about each grandchild and use that knowledge to have fun with them.

*Sometimes:*
- Determine a favorite restaurant for each one.
- Strive to have each grandchild alone from time to time.
- Cut newspaper clippings that you find about their special interests.

*Never:*
- Take a hard look before it is too late!

### 3. Am I comfortable with the way that I handle siblings and cousins when they argue and fight?

*Always:*
- You understand the importance of modeling what you speak.
- You know each of them well enough to understand what is really going on (need for attention, fatigue, jealousy).

*Sometimes:*
- But then there are *those* days!
- Try putting them in separate rooms with books. Talk to them individually until everyone has calmed down and is ready to move on.
- Pick a joint project that everyone has to work on together whenever fighting begins (250-piece puzzle, Lego block project, book with multiple chapters).

*Never:*
- It is better not to be alone with more than one grandchild.

## 3. Do I know my grandchildren's other grandparents?

*Always:*
- If they are important to your grandchildren, they are important to you.

*Sometimes:*
- Ask grandchildren to tell you about them.
- Call to ask their advice on how they handle an issue or a particular *grandchild.*
- Send them notes about your grandparent observations.
- Exchange photographs.

*Never:*
- Time's wasting. Have lunch together or write them a newsy letter.

## Rule 8:
# GRANDPARENTS SHOULD LOVE TO HELP OUT

## LIFESTYLE DIFFERENCES

This rule is simple, straightforward, and true! The fact is, it is *too* true in far *too* many cases. In general, grandparents love to jump in and help out, frequently without even thinking about what they are doing. Perhaps helping out makes them feel needed. Whatever the case, it is a highly seductive invitation.

Most grandparents beg to help. They are dying to help. They expect to help. Because of that, they sometimes go where no grandparent has any right of going!

Of course grandparent assistance of every sort is appreciated, particularly when there is a new grandchild, or when there are several young grandchildren.

> A great deal of family strife might be avoided if the rule said that grandparents should love to offer their help.

Nevertheless, even grandparents with time and enthusiasm on their hands tread on dangerous ground if they presume that helping is their natural right.

Grandparents can avoid having their generous gestures turned into irritations, or even insults, by making sure that all of their offers to help are made before they actually begin to work. Surprise gestures of good-will are not always well timed. As with the child rearing, household helpfulness needs to be at the parent's discretion. Before striking out on helpful missions of mercy of your own, you might want to delve a little deeper into this rule so you can generate a few personal guidelines to keep you in positive territory.

One of the first things that grandparents need to consider is their motivation for wanting to help. The answer to that question can be mixed and can yield some powerful clues:

Some grandparents don't have enough to keep them busy in
their own lives.
Some grandparents are busy, but are concerned for their even
busier adult children.
Some grandparents cannot enter a room without cleaning or
rearranging, so that things meet their own high personal standard.
Some grandparents genuinely dislike how their adult children live
and would love to take steps to set things "right."

It seems that grandparent helpfulness can be spurred on by a variety of stimulants. Helping with housework provides a good example. It can be household clutter or stacks of dirty dishes. It can be messy bedrooms or front lawns that don't get mowed. Whatever the cause, helpful grandparent enthusiasm can easily become misguided reactions to lifestyles that are different from their own.

> The wisest approach for grandparents who are eager to help out is that when in doubt—don't!

When they become parents, adult children take on new responsibilities, but they also acquire new rights. One of these is the right to determine their family's personal lifestyle. Today's families are designing unique solutions to blend busy schedules at work and at home. That can sometimes mean compromising on household chores. Grandparents need to be mindful that the priorities the parents select are not necessarily those that they would choose if the choice was theirs.

One way to combat frustrations with lifestyle differences is by focusing on the things that the parents *are* accomplishing, instead of on the things they don't get around to. By looking closer, grandparents might see that the parents are neglecting the floors, but that they are spending quality time with the grandchildren.

When there is a question of setting priorities and the parents and grandparents have a mismatch, it must be obvious who needs to back down. There are many ways that grandparents can help out, but one of the best is to turn over the control and ask for direction.

Perhaps what the parents would really appreciate is for someone to read to the kids so they can have a quiet cup of tea. Or, a prepared casserole that can be popped into the freezer for a busy day might be the ultimate of all possible gifts. Maybe the parents would enjoy an offer to take home a broken appliance or some torn clothing for repair.

Grandparents who want to help out can offer gift certificates for heavy housework projects like floors and windows, or give vouchers for gardening services. An offer to do midweek grocery shopping or to run an errand could also bring genuine gratitude.

When you leave the boundaries of your own home and come into your grandchildren's homes, you could be most helpful if you learn to pick up a grandchild instead of the dirty dishes, or to give a hug instead of a disapproving glare.

If you are a helpful grandparent who is frustrated by not being allowed to do more, or if you suspect that your helpful offers are causing family tension, it might be time to confess how you feel in order to clear the air. Let the parents know that you have a hard time keeping your hands off their things and out of their business. Tell them that you have only their best interests at heart. Then, be sure to let them know that you intend to defer to their wishes.

# DESIGNING A LIFE OF YOUR OWN

If you could care less about washing someone else's dirty floor, congratulations! You have avoided the pitfalls just mentioned, but you could be in for another kind of trouble. Because this rule says that grandparents should like to help out, you could be seen as uncaring if you don't give cleaning a second thought, and if you avoid doing so as a normal course of action.

Parents might wonder what kind of grandparents could watch them struggle with kids, work, and home chores, day after day, and not jump in to help.

One group might be grandparents who have worked hard all their lives and are finally at the point in life where the children, or at least most of them, are out of the house. As these grandparents sample the joys of the "empty nest," it is possible (perhaps even likely) that they will enjoy this time alone without the intrusions of their children's family obligations and might resist giving up their newfound leisure time in order to help out with chores and errands.

A University of Nebraska task force on family issues in 1992 mentions another group, called the "sandwich generation." These folks are adults around the age of fifty who have children still at home and parents who need some level of their assistance. Grandparents, who have these dual responsibilities are trapped between the two and pulled in both directions so that helping married children with their daily life issues can be more than they can deliver.

That doesn't mean that they don't care. With the uncertainty of knowing if time to themselves will ever come, stress can build up and temper their genuine commitment to help other family members.

When grandparents find themselves on the can't or don't-want-to-help end of the spectrum, it is important that they weigh their priorities realistically and (above all) independently from pressures to feel guilty. Grandparents have the right to determine the terms and conditions of their helpfulness so they can make sure to reserve time to have lives of their own. That is the only way that they can be effective grandparents and suitable life role models.

If grandparents find that they are having difficulties reaching some kind of equilibrium with their own lives and those of their children, they might consider experimenting with some of the following suggestions in order to encourage a more balanced situation:

Be willing to visit instead of always insisting on visits at your home.
Reassure everyone of your willingness to help out in emergencies.
Plan outings with your friends on Sunday afternoons.
Stay alert for the moments when leaving is the best thing to do.
Listen! Listen! Listen!
Keep doing new things.

There is no magic formula for helping just enough but not too much, and being a helpful grandparent will mean different things to different people. Assuming the helpful grandparent role unquestioningly does not allow for the choices that actually do exist.

# SLIPPING AND SLIDING

It might come as a surprise, but being a grandparent doesn't always guarantee that your offers and ideas will be eagerly welcomed. It is important for grandparents to be alert to signs that their view is in opposition to the family's so that they can adjust their behaviors accordingly and contribute to the overall well-being of the family.

If grandparents become too casual in their family interactions, they can let down their guard and engage in risky behaviors. One such behavior is to make frequent, unannounced visits. Another is to criticize the family's routines. If they really want to get on their children's nerves, they can also rearrange belongings, or tell their son or daughter-in-law what their grown child *really* likes to eat.

For a grand finale, they can make sure that they reminisce about the past again and again until everyone knows their stories by heart, and sit and wait by the telephone all week for family members to call and invite them over so that they can do it all again.

A balanced approach to helping out can only come from careful observation, planned conversation, and (realistically) from a period of trial and error. Your home is your domain and that is where you exercise control.

When you ask to lend a helping hand, knowing that the parents believe (from experience) that you will respect their answers, your offers are likely to be received more graciously and with more genuine appreciation.


## EXPLORING RULE 8 CONCEPTS

*Gauge your helpfulness quotient by considering the following questions:*

### 1. Am I satisfied with the level of helpfulness that I lend to my grandchildren's families?

*Always:*
- There is a clear understanding and respect for mutual boundaries.

*Sometimes:*
- Bring a book to read to grandchildren as soon as you arrive. It is a nice habit for them and a safeguard for any urges to clean.
- Have the parents make a wish list of possible household gift certificates.
- Make double recipes on a regular basis (once a week, every two weeks, once a month) and deliver it to their freezer.
- Offer to do shopping from their list (and stick exactly to the list!)

*Never:*
- Ask first.

## 2. Am I satisfied with the limits that have been set about how I will help out?

*Always:*
- Anyway, it is a nonissue.

*Sometimes:*
- Let go of hurt feelings and enjoy your time playing with grand-children.
- If you are not satisfied, give in anyway.
- Do any agreed upon helping quietly and without fanfare.
- Compliment the parents on things that they do well.

*Never:*
- Instead, have grandchildren visit at your home.

## 3. Do I have hobbies and interests that I am excited about?

*Always:*
- Because this is what you deserve!

*Sometimes:*
- Find out what friends are doing and join them at something new.
- Think of ways to share your hobbies with grandchildren (photographs, projects together, outings to shows, and displays of hobbies).
- Share the bounty of your hobbies with grandchildren and their families (vegetables, flowers, pictures, woodwork).

*Never:*
- No excuse!

## 4. Do I do nice things for myself?

*Always:*
- Because you know you are worth it!
- Because it makes you a better grandparent.

*Sometimes:*
- Make a list of three things you would like to do for yourself this week (write a letter, buy some flowers, have a great cup of coffee, talk to an old friend) and post it on the refrigerator. Cross each one out as you do it.
- Invite a friend to a movie.
- Buy a copy of a magazine that you are unfamiliar with.
- Plan to make a favorite (really favorite!) dessert on the first day of each month.

*Never:*
- Still no excuse!

**5. Do I allow the parents to make mistakes without correcting them?**

*Always:*
- You are rare but wise.

*Sometimes:*
- If you regret saying it, take it back!
- If you realize you have interfered, call and tell them that you respect their decision.
- Do not allow the parents or yourself to rake over old coals. If it can't be fixed, forget it.

*Never:*
- Your company is likely not sought after.

## Rule 9:

# GRANDPARENTS SHOULD HATE TO DISCIPLINE

## THE DIRTY "D" WORD

Discipline is an ugly word and the hate-to-discipline rule presents a dilemma for every grandparent. Is there a way for a grandparent to enforce good behavior without being the "bad" guy, or is discipline simply a distasteful chore that has to be gotten through? It is important to dig beneath the surface of this rule in order to see exactly what the implications of its seeming simplicity are.

Without a clear understanding of what an appropriate discipline process is, grandparents will always be tempted to act out of momentary emotion, or to let things slide and just hope for the best.

Any discussion of discipline should begin with an acknowledgment that no discipline is appropriate for infants and toddlers. Their behaviors might annoy the adults around them, but such young children are not capable of misbehaving intentionally. Nor can they remember what they did wrong for any length of time (even for a few minutes!), why they did it, or how they ought to modify their behavior in the future.

Between ages two and five, children acquire the rudiments of self-control and it becomes easier for them to remember when their behavior is inappropriate. Nevertheless, when they are tired or hungry their behavior will often revert to a babyish stage, complete with tactics like yelling and crying. It will be several more years before they are able to delay gratification when things aren't to their liking.

Grandchildren who are school age and adolescents should be a pleasure to spend time with. Over the years, grandparents will have to exert less and less control over their behavior. They will be able to rely on their grandchildren's growing abilities to make better and better judgments, which is the ultimate goal of any discipline approach!

Certainly, no grandparent wants to waste precious time during visits scolding and punishing their grandchildren.

Actually, this rule says what every grandparent believes deep down; that they hate having to discipline their grandchildren. That is good. It would make no sense for grandparents to want to take on this role that rightfully belongs to the parents. Still, that doesn't quite get to the heart of the issue.

> Grandparents are supposed to be sweet, loving, and kind. Grandchildren are supposed to be respectful, quiet, and obedient. (And whoever believes that is neither a grandparent nor a grandchild!)

When all is said and done, what grandparents generally dislike is the effect of scolding and punishing. Acting as the enforcer makes them feel terrible. Even worse, it appears to make their grandchildren resentful and angry at them. Tears, sour looks, and scornful remarks are painful interruptions to the bonding process that grandparents work so hard to build. Yet, if grandparents love their grandchildren, they know (deep down) that they have to insist on appropriate behavior from them.

If you accept the premise that grandparents hate to punish, but you care about your grandchildren, you can determine what sorts of compromises you are willing to make with your feelings in order to get the job done. You can find ways to teach important lessons in positive ways, minimizing emotional reactions that fail to reach the heart of the matter.

# GETTING THE RESULTS
# THAT YOU WANT

Are there ways to induce perfect behavior when grandchildren are with you so that you don't have to discipline? Perfect behavior? Probably not. Close to perfect? Quite possibly.

With some simple modifications in the ways you view behavior control, you can eliminate most of the troublesome areas and disciplinary dilemmas that you face. If you are willing to take this rule apart and see it for what it is, you will be pleased to discover that it isn't really a case of hating to discipline. What you face is a case of learning to enjoy molding your grandchildren's behavior in positive ways so that you can all enjoy each of them more completely.

These ends can be accomplished by deciding ahead of time how you are going to react to inappropriate behavior, instead of responding emotionally at the time of the incident. (Which frequently means adult behaviors that are as inappropriate as the child's, such as scolding, threatening, and yelling.)

Appropriate discipline can make you feel better as a grandparent and is well worth your efforts, as long as you accept that you need to train yourself, as well as your grandchildren. Consider any of the following approaches and build your response repertoire from them as you become a more proficient but firm grandparent.

- **Alter how you view your role in the discipline process.** Discipline is not something that you need to deliver or impose. Try viewing discipline as an action that the child chooses so that the responsibility for good behavior rests with the child, not with you. You are there to assist in helping the grandchildren learn how to make good choices. They are the learners who choose to learn.
- **Set up clear choice and consequence plans.** Grandchildren need predictability in order to learn and modify their behavior. Good discipline begins with helping them to understand what it is that you (or other adults) expect from them. By setting a few simple rules and explaining what the consequence will be if they *choose* to ignore them, the mystery of misbehavior is removed. Remember that when you feel the need for a rule at their house or at yours, consensus with the parents is a must if it is going to work.
- **Let grandchildren help to design the system.** Supporting the discipline system is a must, so when grandchildren are old enough to reason and remember, it is best if they help to design the system with you, including the punishments. Most grandchildren will bask in glory at this newfound grown-up responsibility.

No longer will you need to be a crabby grandparent who is scolding and punishing. When the discipline system is clear, grandchildren are not disobeying you, they are disobeying their own rules and earning their own agreed-upon consequences. It no longer makes sense to call you mean. They have to put the blame where it belongs, and you can even offer your condolences as they accept their own punishment.

Here is an example of how this works. Say that your granddaughter constantly takes juice into the living room, even though you have asked her not to do so. She spills the juice and this makes you angry. You decide that enough is enough and you ask her not to take it in there anymore and to come up with a punishment if she does it again.

She suggests that she will have to clean up the mess and drink at the kitchen table for the rest of the day. Later in the day, she breaks the rule again. You ask her to tell you what the consequence is that she agreed to. She proceeds to clean up the juice and moves to the kitchen table, without your having to have an argument about it. You have shifted the burden to your granddaughter. Instead of being the enforcer, you have become the teacher/mentor.

- **Use only a few, simple rules.**   With young children, it is important to keep rules simple. Begin with those areas that are really important to you. If screaming drives you up the walls, make a rule about how loud voices should be when grandchildren are at your house. The same goes with behaviors like arguing, tattling, or hitting. Other rules might include listing items in the house that are for adult use only (stereos, remote controls), or areas that are off limits for safety or personal reasons.

When you have a few simple rules, you are ready to discuss them together and link them to specific consequences. Hitting might result in having to sit in grandma's chair for five minutes. Fighting over toys might mean having to give up the toy and read a book with grandpa.

Consequences do not have to feel bad in order to succeed, but they do need to break the misbehavior cycle. The older grandchildren get, the less success you will have from making them suffer, anyway, because they will remember and hold a grudge!

> When designing consequences, remember that the idea isn't to make grandchildren suffer. It is to make them behave so that your time together can be more enjoyable.

- **Idle threats have no place in discipline.** If you aren't willing to follow up with the designated consequence, don't threaten to do so. If you say you will cancel the trip to Disneyland if your grandson acts up one more time, be prepared to act accordingly and to bear the consequences of enforcing your own words.
- **Offer choices for minor difficulties.** It is not always necessary to react strongly to misbehavior. When behaviors are minor annoyances rather than real problems, consider offering choices instead of rushing ahead and punishing. Choice techniques are well worth learning for a number of reasons. They require no lengthy study to understand and learn. They work well with any age, right up to and including adults, and best of all, they make sense!

Each of us is continually involved in the process of making decisions throughout our daily lives. Making decisions is a good thing because it puts us in control and gives us greater personal freedom. It would not be any fun to go to a restaurant and to be told what we can have to eat. The pleasure in dining out is as much in the choosing as in the eating.

The same is true with grandchildren. When someone asks them what they think, it makes them feel respected and valued. Unfortunately, adults frequently shortchange children by not allowing them the benefit of the countless opportunities to make choices that occur as they interact together.

If you are like most adults, you probably direct grandchildren in dozens of small ways in order to keep things calm and controlled. It is just easier, as the argument goes. Offering choices is a great way to promote calmer visits, while at the same time helping your grandchildren to practice learning valuable choosing skills. Choosing is a learned behavior. It would be nice if we were born knowing how to do it, but that just isn't so. When you offer choices, everyone wins. You avoid a battle, your grandchildren learn new skills, and their self-esteem is given a big boost.

Consider the following choice examples and think of ways to incorporate similar choice questions into your own grandparenting interactions.

*Example 1*
Your granddaughter is headed for the wall with crayons. You can (a) scream and pull her away, or (b) say, "Would you like to color at the table or on the porch?"

*Example 2*

Your grandson is ready to tear up your new golf magazine. You can (a) grab it away, or (b) say, "Do you want to tear up some newspapers, or some bags?"

*Example 3*

One grandchild wants something that the other is playing with. You can (a) yell at them both to stop fighting, threatening to take all the toys away, or (b) ask the intruder, "Do you want to help me cut up vegetables for dinner, or would you like to sit in my lap and color?"

By giving grandchildren opportunities to make choices, you give them a chance to learn valuable lessons about responsibility and to think logically when they make decisions.

## Anticipate Trouble

There may be certain times, or certain places that bring out undesirable behaviors in grandchildren. If you can identify and avoid them, you would be well ahead in the discipline game.

For example, if driving in the car is a problem, put together a small box of crackers and toys to hand out as each car trip begins. Or, if you are going to have to wait in a long line at the bank, bring along a friend to take your grandchild on a walk while you complete your banking errand.

## Give Gentle Reminders

When you see a difficult situation arising, prepare your grandchild to cope with it before it happens. A gentle, non-nagging reminder often works well with preschoolers and older children when it comes to preventing behavior problems. For example, it can help to remind grandchildren not to run before you open the door and let them into the store. Or, before you go through the checkout line, you may want to remind your grandchildren that there are cookies in the grocery basket but that they cannot have the candy at the checkout counter.

## Inject Humor

With older children, a little humor can go a long way toward diffusing troublesome situations. It works especially well with older grandchildren as it allows them to save face when they are wrong.

## Overlook Small Annoyances

Sometimes it really is easier to ignore small infractions like whining or nagging, particularly if your time with grandchildren is limited. To determine if this is one of those times, ask yourself some of these guiding questions in order to help measure your response:

Is there a health or safety issue?

Is there an important value at stake?

Are you worried about what others will think?

Is the child breaking a household rule?

Is this a knee-jerk reaction on your part?

Can the child learn something as a result of following
   the path they are on?

## Use Positive Phrases

Sometimes reversing a negative behavior can be as simple as stating positively what you wish done. "Please do this," will usually work better than striking out with, "Don't do that." Or, "I like it when you clean up," generally draws a more favorable response than, "Stop making messes!"

## Discuss the Issue

If the behavior includes just one child, you can model good problem solving by taking the time to sit down and talk things out before you act.

If the problem involves more than one grandchild, try facilitating a discussion to find out what has happened, and how each person is feeling as a result. It is always best if grandchildren can resolve their own conflicts instead of having to rely on adults to do it for them. Until they are old enough to be reasonable, they might need guidance in the process.

## Reinforce Good Behavior

One of the very best disciplinary approaches you can use is to reinforce and draw attention to your grandchildren's positive acts (of which there are an abundance!). It is far too easy to draw attention only to what goes wrong when grandchildren seek and need positive feedback from loved ones.

There are an unlimited number of ways to reinforce good behavior. Verbal praise is an easy one to deliver, as is food (if used in moderation). Experiment to see what works best by rewarding with special activities, or one-on-one attentions. Other methods could include giving tokens, such as plastic chips that can be redeemed for trips, goodies, or special activities. And don't forget that children always thrive on hugs and smiles!

# EXPLORING RULE 9 CONCEPTS

*The following statements can help you to get started designing discipline reactions that put you in control:*

## 1. Do I have clear expectations of my grandchildren's behavior?

*Always:*
- You also have a clear understanding of developmental expectations.
- If things are working, they have a clear understanding of your expectations, too.

*Sometimes:*
- Review developmental guidelines for a grandchild's next stage. Keep one step ahead.
- When you feel things are getting out of control, jot down what is making you mad. Pinpoint problem areas and make changes to routines that could affect their behavior (help with toy cleanup, provide an extra snack, keep sweets out of sight, limit television viewing, go to the bank tomorrow).
- Anticipate hunger and fatigue. Monitor times and places that they occur.

*Never:*
- Things could get pretty chaotic.

## 2. Do I feel that the parents are too lenient or too strict?

*Always:*
- Expressing your displeasure is unlikely to help and could make matters worse.

*Sometimes:*
- Give them the gift of a good parenting or discipline book. (Suggestions can be found under Grandparent Resources in the Appendix.)
- Recognize that they probably feel the same about you!
- Take consolation in the fact that new parents relax over time.

*Never:*
- Consider yourself lucky and enjoy your great relationships!

### 3. Do my grandchildren embarrass me in public?

*Always:*
- Let the parents know (gently, if that is possible) why you wish to play with them at home.

*Sometimes:*
- Give grandchildren gentle reminders that your standard is different from their parents when you are with them in public.
- Remind grandchildren of your expectations before going out. Return home if necessary.
- Avoid friends when you are out.

*Never:*
- Enjoy sharing the world with them!

### 4. Do I follow through when I make a threat?

*Always:*
- Good. Your grandchildren know that when you say something, you mean it.

*Sometimes:*
- Without consistency, a threat is just an order ready made to challenge.
- Be careful not to make threats (we will leave here if you don't stop . . .) unless you are able to carry them out.
- Children tend to remember the exception, not the rule.

*Never:*
- Talk away. You are wasting your breath.

### 5. Do I believe that discipline should teach, not punish?

*Always:*
- Your discipline measures will have positive consequences.

*Sometimes:*
- Remember that in spite of love and the best of intentions, it is normal for young children to get on your nerves.
- Although when they make you angry, the distinction can become more hazy.
- When you are getting emotional, remind yourself what you are trying to teach.
- Never discipline when you are angry.

*Never:*
- You can expect grandchildren to push you to the limits!

## 6. Can I overlook small annoyances?

*Always:*
- Always?

*Sometimes:*
- Figure out what your triggers are and avoid exposing them (whining, arguing, ignoring directions, screaming).
- Practice makes perfect—really!
- Look at the big picture. Have they behaved pretty well the rest of the time? Are they hungry, bored, or tired?

*Never:*
- Make sure the parents are around to help you out.

## Rule 10:
# GRANDPARENTS SHOULD KNOW HOW TO CARE FOR SICK KIDS

## CALLS FOR HELP

If you are like most grandparents, it is likely that you will receive a panicky phone call someday asking you for advice for a grandchild who is sick. Coping with childhood illness is a difficult challenge for new parents, for it can be frightening to be in charge of a small child who is feverish or delirious. The first few times can test shaky parent skills.

The call will probably transport you back to your own early parenting days when you were faced with the sometimes overwhelming responsibility of dealing with sick children. Unfortunately, those experiences make it seem natural for grandparents to chime in with helpful directions, even though it may be decades since they faced similar situations.

Before grandparents rush in to get things under control, they may want to think about what they are going to do in response to a request for medical assistance.

Being asked to give counsel regarding illness is undoubtedly one of the highest forms of flattery that a grandparent can receive!

It is nothing less than an all-encompassing vote of confidence in you! That is all well and good, but how should you respond? You could (a) share old family remedies, or (b) give into a rising sense of panic and freeze up, or (c) offer reassurances and advise the parents to call their pediatrician.

Hopefully, you will fall into the group that suggests reaching for the telephone and calling the pediatrician, even though that could mean toning down the flattery and resisting offers of advice. There are some very good reasons for doing this. As you examine this rule further, you may well become a firm believer that a better role for you to play is that of the cheerleader, instead of aspiring to be the team captain.

It is good to avoid the first group, because giving medical advice can be risky; a risk you should not want to take. Medical practices have changed since you were a parent. Furthermore, giving advice and directions can undermine the parent's confidence in their own ability to cope with family emergencies.

If grandparents really want to help, they can consider giving parents a good medical reference book as a gift. Two especially comprehensive ones include the *American Medical Association Complete Guide to Your Children's Health and Complete Baby* and *Child Care* by Dr. Miriam Stoppard.

Young parents can be embarrassed by having to call the doctor for advice. A good reference book might get them through the more common questions and bouts of illness that will certainly occur. Grandparents can assure parents that pediatric staff are trained to respond to the concerns of new parents, that such calls are an expected part of their practice, and that there is no such thing as a stupid question!

Not everything has changed when it comes to caring for sick children. For one thing we now have fairly compelling evidence that chicken soup might actually be good for a cold, and that alternative treatments like herbs and massage can be effective in treating symptoms. But while much of what was done when you were a parent remains the same, sorting out what is different could be a perilous undertaking.

# SHAPING HEALTHY ATTITUDES

An excellent way for grandparents to contribute to their grandchildren's health is to demonstrate healthy lifestyle attitudes. This can be done even if they don't live near their grandchildren. What grandparents model in their own health habits is internalized by their grandchildren, even when they aren't discussed!

As a grandparent, you can talk about some of the healthy things that you do, like taking walks every day, or passing up on high-fat foods. You can send grandchildren surprise packages with snazzy new toothbrushes and rolls of flavored dental floss.

If you live close enough, you can help out by taking grandchildren to preventive dental and medical appointments. Families today are busy and this kind of assistance can allow working parents to save time off for more serious illnesses.

# WHEN BABY COMES EARLY

The American Association for Premature Infants notes that about 10% of newborns (over 400,000 babies) are born premature every year, which means before the eighth month of pregnancy is completed. Premature babies are either low birth weight of three to five pounds, or very low birth weight of under three pounds.

Babies in the first group do very well with over 90% having no visible lasting effects. Babies in the second group are being treated more effectively now than ever before, with 75% of them bearing no visible or lasting effects. Problems that do persist are usually mild and include things such as near-sightedness and learning disabilities, both of which respond to treatment.

Having a premature baby is one of the most stressful experiences that a parent can have. Most parents find it very difficult to go through the experience of having their baby in a neonatal intensive care unit without some form of emotional support. The sight of infants hooked up to tubes and wires in an incubator is a frightening sight. The parents can't pick the baby up to hold or cuddle, and the baby might even lack the appearance and features that make babies appear to be "cute." Getting through the difficult stage requires assurance from people, like grandparents, that the baby will look more normal as weight is gained and the health is stabilized.

Stroking an arm or leg can provide good stimulation and conveys love in the absence of holding and cuddling. Research shows that even twenty minutes a day of such touching can have a noticeable positive effect.

Stereotypical attitudes that premature infants are less cute, smaller, and less likable are not true and grandparents can try to guard against them in their interactions with the grandchildren and parents. Interacting with premature babies might not seem as rewarding at this time, but if everyone perseveres, the grandchild will catch up and become its own wonderful little person in no time!

Grandparents can assist the parents of premature babies through the attitudes they project, as it is possible that the parents are not experiencing the normal joyful feelings that accompany the birth of new children. There can be continual worry about what lies ahead, as well as concerns for the child's healthy survival. Add to that the stress of having to deal with a host of nurses, doctors, other health care professionals, and insurance claims, and this is likely to equate to a struggle for everyone in the family.

If the baby must remain in the hospital for an extended period of time, family dynamics can be challenged even further. On top of worrying about the child's health, there can be guilt and doubt about the cause of the child's premature birth. There can also be underlying feelings of general inadequacy as a result of the situation. And finally, it is normal for parents to feel angry that the birth was not smooth and trouble free, like those of friends and family members.

From the outside, grandparents know that such things are the manifestations of stress and fatigue. Being aware of these feelings, and acting supportively in what they say and do, can help the parents emerge from the traumatic situation in an emotionally healthy way. If there are siblings, this may be the ideal time to step in and help out with child care so the parents can get out occasionally to relax.

## Coping with Colic

Colic is common in premature babies, but it is also seen in about one out of five full-term infants according to the Wellness Interactive Network. When an infant has colic, there is a great deal of inconsolable crying, accompanied by writhing and screaming. These behaviors are persistent, severe, and typically last for more than three hours each day. Colic is not an illness, as such, and usually goes away by the age of four months.

There is almost nothing more upsetting to a parent or grandparent than listening to a continually crying child. Nature designed us to react to crying so that we pay attention to an infant's needs, but when the crying child can't be comforted, it can become nearly intolerable to be around, trying the patience of even the most loving caregiver.

There are many theories as to why babies develop colic, none of which are conclusive. Ten to 15% of babies are born colicky and both breast- and bottle-fed babies are equally subject. There is no predominance by ethnicity or gender, although babies who are born prematurely are slightly more prone to colic.

Soothing the baby is not easy and usually involves a trial-and-error approach to find out what works best for each particular colicky child. Some things recommended by the Wellness Network that work for many parents include:

strapping the baby close to the body

riding in a car

placing the baby near a running washer, dryer, or vacuum

soft music

gentle back massages with the baby lying on its
  tummy across the adult's knees

pacifiers

plastic nursing bottles with collapsible bags

None of these techniques work all the time and in all cases and a certain amount of prolonged crying still needs to be endured.

Adult coping mechanisms are equally important so that the child is not inadvertently rejected. The parents will benefit from the grandparent's assurance that the crying is not their fault and that they haven't failed to provide adequate care. Parents may need reassurance that it is also not the pediatrician's fault, and there is no magic prescription that can be administered to stop the crying.

# THE LONG AND SHORT OF IT

Grandchildren come in all shapes and sizes, but large infants can turn into petite adults and small ones can ultimately tower over other family members. There are genetic surprises in all families, with siblings appearing and acting quite differently, and cousins sometimes seeming more like siblings.

By focusing on what is unique in each grandchild and not labeling those differences as "better," "slower," or "nicer," grandparents allow each child a fair chance to grow in an atmosphere that is nurturing and completely accepting.

Differences and individualities are well worth celebrating. Grandparents can promote family peace of mind if they avoid comparisons (even obvious ones) between other children or other grandchildren. All children have individual developmental timetables that are set biologically, making comparisons meaningless, anyway. If a grandparent spends a great deal of time with their grandchildren and notices an area where development seems to be lagging, they should certainly bring it to the parent's attention, but by and large differences reflect no more than mere maturational diversity.

The greatest gift that a grandparent can give each grandchild who comes into their lives is to respect and appreciate the personality and individuality within in as many ways as possible!

# TALKING DILEMMAS

If you are lucky enough to live near young grandchildren, you will undoubtedly wait expectantly for the first recognizable word, an event that should occur somewhere between the first and second birthday. The flow of words to follow will be a joy for all of the family.

Sometimes, a child is a late talker. If a grandchild refuses to talk, there is no need to be overly concerned as long as the child understands most of what is being said and follows simple directions. Some very bright children refuse to talk until as late as age three, at which time they gush forth with lengthy and complete grammatically correct sentences. However, as a precaution, the child who has not begun talking by age three should be evaluated to rule out any physical causes for the situation.

It is important for adults to model good grammar and pronunciation during the language development stage. Baby talk is fine for young infants, but does not further learning in older infants, toddlers, and preschoolers.

If grandparents are with their young grandchildren on a frequent basis, they can contribute significantly to the development of good language by using consistent language modeling. Toddlers will make up cute words, but it is best to resist the urge to repeat them back. The correct words are really what grandchildren need to hear during this period of rapid language acquisition.

A system of grammar evolves naturally over time and a self-correcting process for abnormalities happens all by itself during the early school years. Grandparents know from experience that this built-in language system is at work and they can enjoy the charm of this entertaining early talk instead of fretting over incorrect pronunciations, or incorrect sentence structure.

Finally, grandparents should have as much patience as possible when they are around young grandchildren who are practicing their new talking skills. Their chatter can seem endless, and it can be better to limit time together rather than to ask them to be quiet.

Few things are more demoralizing to the young, experimenting talker than to be told that they are annoying the important people in their lives with their new skill.

By listening attentively, grandparents can promote a bridge of communication that will last far into the future and enhance all of their grandparenting efforts and relationships.

# SERIOUS ILLNESS

All children experience a certain amount of childhood illness, but a serious or chronic illness that lasts for months or longer is an unexpected and dreaded event for any grandparent. The idea of caring for a seriously ill child is not usually the issue as much as the difficulty in seeing a young child helpless and in discomfort.

Some of the more common serious childhood conditions that occur include things like asthma, epilepsy (neurological irregularities), cardiac conditions, orthopedic problems, and diabetes. These chronic conditions can be accompanied by episodes of acute illness, as well as by ongoing chronic symptoms that influence the daily regimen of everyone in the family.

Grandparents can assist in a number of concrete ways, all of which are active alternatives that are more productive than merely fretting and becoming more upset.

## Help the Parents to Explain Things to the Child

One of the most important things to remember when dealing with a child who is chronically ill is that the child is still a child like any other child, in terms of curiosity and need for behavior control. This can only come about when they are treated like the individuals that they are, and told about what is happening to them.

Depending on the age of the child, explanations tailored to the child's level will help to lessen the fears of mystery and vulnerability. Accepting the child's feelings, handling fears openly, and being supportive but not overly indulgent, are useful grandparent and family approach tactics.

## Tell the Child How They Can Help Out

In general, children seem to accept treatments and medications better if they understand what is going on and how they can cooperate.

Preparation about treatments that are upcoming can also help to reduce the anxiety of medical visits and hospitalization. When children are seriously ill, their behavior should be expected to be more demanding, but knowledge and understanding can help to lessen, or even ward off continual difficult behavior.

## Treat the Child as Normally as Possible

The desire to coddle and protect are natural, but the family, grandparents included, have to weigh the results of giving in to all of the child's requests. As hard as it can seem, the child needs as much of the same treatment as possible as the other members of the family. Additional affection is always appropriate, but forgetting to treat a child like a child is not.

## Help Find Ways to Dispel Boredom

Boredom can be a problem, especially if the child is bedridden. Grandparents can spend time reading to the child and listening to records and tapes. If the grandparents cannot be there in person, they can still help by recording and mailing them to sick grandchildren.

Talking or playing simple board and card games will also enable visits to feel more enjoyable and productive. If grandchildren feel well enough, a simple craft activity like coloring, molding play dough, or making simple hand puppets will also be highly enjoyable, especially when done with the grandparent.

## EXPLORING RULE 10 CONCEPTS

*Review the following concepts to understand your feelings about grandparent medical interventions:*

### 1. Do I have current infant CPR and first-aid certification?

*Always:*
- This is a worthwhile area to devote time to.
- You may never use these skills, but at least you will not have to look back after an accident knowing you could have had them!

*Sometimes:*
- Consider updating if yours has expired.
- If you have one and not the other, consider going all the way.
- Take a friend along and make a day of it, complete with a congratulatory lunch or dinner.

*Never:*
- If you do it now for the first time, you will wish you had done this years ago.

## 2. Do I express confidence in the parents' abilities to deal with regular childhood illness?

*Always:*
- You have probably given them one of the good resource books mentioned in this rule. (Suggestions can be found under Grandparent Resources in the Appendix.)

*Sometimes:*
- A few encouraging words can calm a parent. Sometimes, they just need to be reminded.
- If you feel advice coming on, remind them that it has been a long time since you were a parent.
- Remind them that you practically lived in your pediatrician's office!

*Never:*
- This could be going too far in the opposite direction!

## 3. Do I refrain from making comparisons (negative or positive) to other children and grandchildren?

*Always:*
- You have learned to appreciate the diversity of young children.

*Sometimes:*
- Remember that even good comparisons create expectations that might not fit the child.
- Appreciate and respect what the child can do now and resist the urge to push them on.
- Reassure parents whose children are developing on an atypical schedule or rate.

*Never:*
- Remember that new parents can be prone to exaggerating possibilities.

## 4. Do I nag parents about health habits that may not really be important (bare feet, runny noses, lack of heavy clothing)?

*Always:*
- You have mastered the ability to look the other way!

*Sometimes:*
- Consider if an old wives' tale might be at work.

- If the house is warm, ignore the bare feet.
- Not every child is cold-blooded; particularly when they are outside running about.
- There are more germs in a heated closed room than in the backyard.

*Never:*
- They are probably ignoring what you say anyway.

## Rule 11:
# BRAGGING SHOULD BE DONE IN MODERATION

## HITTING HIGH NOTES

As you read this rule, your shoulders may sag and your gaze may fall to the ground. After all, bragging is tantamount to grandparenting! There are few grandparents who would not gladly break this rule, and probably do so with regularity already! Despite this, there seems to be a widespread (but generally unspoken) understanding that excessive grandparent bragging is an undesirable trait, regardless of how special, talented, or adorable the grandchildren are.

Such a shame! Grandparents who brag too much are apt to be reminded that they have crossed this invisible line, even as they are just getting warmed up. Perhaps, the first task for attempting to operate under the restrictions of this rule is to determine what the acceptable limits for grandparent bragging are. (Only then can you figure out how to get around them!)

There will rarely be an objection if you brag by passing around photos carried in your wallet, although there is some question as to whether you should be requested to do so, or whether you can accidentally spill them out onto the floor. Likewise, you can count on being politely indulged when you tell one cute story, you should expect resistance if you launch into a second, let alone a third such tale!

This tight-fisted rule frequently gets in the way of proud grandparents, putting them on the defensive. Your strong feelings of pride and joy are bursting to get out, but have to be measured and meted out in drips and trickles, as social conventions dictate. (And this, when you could go on for hours if you could just hold your audience captive!)

The question remaining is if there is a way for you to square your desires to brag without endangering your chances to continue to receive invitations to dinners and other social events? In short, can you flaunt all the great things that you are holding inside of you without being ostracized from your social circles?

You can break this rule and neatly circumvent it by developing methods of bragging that are unexpected and innovative. You can learn to catch all of your friends off guard before they can cut you off. Not only is such a feat possible, it is fairly easy to do.

> If you are clever, there are many ways to evade this rule while appearing to honor its conventions!

Once you have covered standard bragging methods like pictures in the wallet, photo albums on the coffee table, and photo key chains, it is time to move into the next dimension of grandparent crowing. Your grandchildren are talented enough to provide you with ample raw material, so let go and begin to plan some exciting new ways to display their charms and talents as no grandparent has done before!

# CREATIVE WAYS TO BRAG

There are unlimited ways to go about bragging once you begin to focus on the unusual. You might want to begin with a few of the ideas suggested below to get you started. Variations will undoubtedly spring up as you progress.

## Hold a Family Art Show

Reserve a Saturday or Sunday afternoon (well in advance, so all of the important participants can be there) and send out invitations for a formal family art show and reception. Plan special refreshments and request that the guests (family and friends) come in dressy attire so that your grandchildren will feel like the honored guests that they are. Decorate with fresh flowers and put out the best china and silver.

To prepare for the show, collect artwork from each of your grandchildren, including the infants. (Yes, scribbles are artwork, too!) Frame the art pieces using colored construction or poster paper from an art store. Place a large gold award sticker on your favorite piece from each grandchild, and attach a tag noting the special category that the art piece is being honored for.

Your toddlers could be acclaimed for *Best Efforts by a Baby,* and your eight-year-old grandson for his *Best Drawing of a Racing Car.* Why not honor *Best Interpretation of Life by a Teenager?* Include artwork from every grandchild and take lots of pictures on the day of the event so you can make a memory book and mail photos to out of town grandchildren who cannot be there in person.

Imagine being the proud grandparents of so many fine young artists!

## Host a Music Recital

If you have grandchildren who are musicians, even beginners, why not host a formal music recital in their honor? This could also make a good dress-up affair with printed invitations and fancy refreshments.

On the day of the event, have printed programs (easily done on a computer) with the names of the musical piece to be performed, along with the name of the grandchild performing it. If there are adults in the family who play instruments, consider an intergenerational duet as a special grand finale.

This event can give your family and friends a chance to enjoy your homegrown talent while it allows your budding musicians to experience performing in a live, nonthreatening environment. You might even want to make it an annual event.

## Create an Art Gallery in Your Home

Hanging your grandchildren's artwork on the refrigerator is great, but you can do better than that! With a little extra effort, you can show off how proud you are of your grandchildren's artistic accomplishments on a permanent basis.

Watch for frame sales at local art and frame shops and purchase some nice ones that match your decor, along with matting cut to fit inside of them. Select a prominent and visible place in your home and measure off a space to arrange the frames for your grandchildren's art gallery. Consider mounting a spotlight to focus on the artwork.

Let your grandchildren know that you are doing this and have them send you lots of their favorite drawings and paintings as they create them. Place them in the matted frames, along with a tag listing the child's name and age at the time of the creation. Once your grandchildren see your gallery, they will be more than happy to restock your supply with new pieces and you will discover (along with all of your guests) that artwork created by grandchildren is actually quite stunning!

Your friends and acquaintances will be treated to a rotating art display, and you won't have to drag them past the refrigerator anymore. Best of all, your grandchildren will be extremely proud to see how much you value the artwork that they create for you!

## Wear a Photo Shirt

Custom T-shirt design shops can take ordinary photographs of your grandchildren and enlarge them onto T-shirts. You might even consider wearing a collage of several, or all of your grandchildren on the same shirt.

Displaying your grandchildren so openly makes a strong visual statement to your very special little ones. Even better, you won't have to ask if anyone wants to see a picture of them!

## Stitch a Memory Pillow

If you can locate fabric scraps from your grandchildren's early outfits and infant blankets, you can piece them together with some lace trim to make a grandbaby memory pillow for your sofa. Or, use scraps from Halloween costumes, birthdays, and sports team shirts. Or, use other special outfits and let your imagination guide you.

Foam pillow forms are available at fabric stores to use as foundations. When friends visit and sit down, they cannot help but notice your colorful creations, giving you the perfect opening for some treasured grandparent stories.

## Start a Grandchild Measuring Post

An out-of-the-way wall is fine, or use a strip of wood at least six and a half feet tall to make a measuring post. Mark the height of each grandchild with an indelible pen at regular intervals, adding the dates, beginning as early in their lives as possible. (Yes, you can lay grandbabies flat and stretch them out gently to get a "height.") Continue until they are all full-grown high school graduates and you will have a treasure of memories that everyone will be drawn to whenever they visit your home.

## Build a Coffee Table Book

A coffee table scrapbook can be used to store memorabilia so that it is close at hand when you feel a spell of bragging coming on. These are wonderful if you can start them when they are infants, but there is no reason why you cannot begin one with older grandchildren, whose lives are still full of memorable events, awards, photos, letters, and cards.

Include things like schoolwork, photographs, lists of their favorite books, special letters written to you, teachers' notes and report cards, and drawings on which they dictate stories about their pictures.

The more creative you become with this rule, the better you can evade it without getting a reputation among your peers as an overbearing grandparent. Best of all, everyone in your family will know that you are the proudest grandparent around!

# EXPLORING RULE 11 CONCEPTS

*Consider if you are taking your bragging rights to their limit:*

## 1. Do I carry photographs of grandchildren in my wallet?

*Always:*
- Of course!

*Sometimes:*
- This hit-and-miss approach is wasting time.
- You cannot adequately return in kind when other grandparents show you theirs.

*Never:*
- You must not carry a wallet.

## 2. Do I enjoy hearing about my friends' grandchildren?

*Always:*
- And after listening attentively, you return the favor.

*Sometimes:*
- All grandparents should be able to identify and have fun with grandparent stories.
- If you make the time for them, they owe you the reverse.

*Never:*
- Too bad! All children should be loved and appreciated.

## 3. Do I encourage skills and abilities in my grandchildren?

*Always:*
- You understand the need for new raw (bragging) material!

*Sometimes:*
- Opportunities are slipping through your fingers.

- Their new interests can spark bragging possibilities that you haven't even considered yet!

*Never:*

- Your refrigerator is probably decorated with spelling and math worksheets. Put something exciting up there!

## 4. Do I encourage all grandchildren to share with me?

*Always:*

- And that includes thoughts as well as creations.
- It also includes major and minor news.

*Sometimes:*

- Listen carefully to what grandchildren are saying to see what they are currently excited about.
- Reward grandchildren with your attention.
- The better you listen, the more they will open up and share with you.

*Never:*

- The relationships sound way too one-sided.

# BEING A GRANDPARENT IS ALWAYS FUN

## BUT JUST IN CASE IT ISN'T

This rule has been left for last because it is, by far, the most difficult. It is so difficult that it would be nice to omit it altogether, but that would be dishonest. Of course grandparenting is fun. No self-respecting grandparent wants it to be any other way. However, like life itself, grandparenting has no written guarantees and difficult challenges can, and do, sometimes arise.

This rule asks grandparents to reaffirm their belief that bad things won't happen to their grandchildren. Seeing a tiny new grandbaby for the first time, even if only from a distance in a photograph, makes the need for that belief even stronger. In those first moments, what grandparent does not affirm that if they have anything to do with it, this child's life will go smoothly?

It is almost as if part of being a grandparent is to stand vigilant guard and wish bad things away. The grandparent commitment to each grandchild is that strong!

Parents also feel this obligation as part of their natural bonding process with the child, but grandparents experience it from a different perspective. The grandparent perspective on "bad" times stems from experiencing and looking back on the difficulties of a lifetime. Grandparents know, firsthand, that the unspeakable *does* sometimes happen. This rule, which seems so light on the surface, challenges grandparents to focus on the positive while acknowledging that they are ready and willing to do whatever is necessary in the event that difficulties do arise.

When this rule is seen as an intention to be a vigilant but silent guard, it is a good rule. It recognizes that life can be harsh, while affirming the desire that only good things come into a grandchild's life. If it is viewed as an absolute truth, it can become the denial of one who cannot face and survive difficult grandparent challenges.

Challenges are nothing new to grandparents. By virtue of the fact that they have experienced a great deal of life and survived, it is likely that they have developed the resources needed to handle what comes their way as grandparents. It should be comforting to know that one has the fortitude and skills to face what comes, while at the same time working toward happiness as the goal.

In the overwhelming majority of cases, with the overwhelming majority of grandparents, grandparenting is fun; a great deal of fun, in fact! But given the frustrating complexities of today's world, a fair number of grandparents can count on occasional rough times with adult children and/or confused grandchildren. Like it or not, grandparents are often seen at these times as the clan leaders, and they may be approached for involvement, if not solutions.

At other times, grandparents can be viewed as having the financial resources or time to fix difficult situations, neither of which should be automatically presumed to be true.

> The question that arises with any family problem is how much grandparents owe, either of themselves or their resources, to resolving family problems.

The answer to that question has plagued many a distraught grandparent, for there is no magic formula or definitive answer.

It could be argued that part of being a strong grandparent is to step back and let the parents solve their own problems when they are able. Depending on the nature of the problem, and the likelihood that it will repeat, that could be true. It might be equally important for grandparents to accept that they won't always be around to bail children or grandchildren out. Sometimes, a hard lesson is necessary to save them from later pain.

Another view of grandparent involvement is that, having passed through the trials of parenthood themselves, they have earned the right to a stage of life removed from the continual problems and the stress that go along with raising a family. When a grandparent's health is an issue, this certainly makes sense. It seems fair that a grandparent has the right to guard their own physical and mental health. Perhaps they are not equipped to give limitlessly of anything but their love and encouragement.

Family conflicts can release an enormous amount of anger from everyone involved. When the issue is with the parents, grandparents can still reach out to the affected grandchildren to provide some sense of continuity. Young children, in particular, tend to equate the amount of time adults spend with them with the amount that they are loved.

> During difficult family times, when parents are hurting and need more time alone, it can be confusing to the children to have less of their time. Grandparents can fill that void in very real ways.

Continual demonstrations of love from grandparents can reinforce for grandchildren that they are not at fault, that it is acceptable to feel angry, and that they can let other adults know how they feel. When grandparents work directly with their grandchildren to ease their stress, the parents frequently benefit, as well.

Until the 1980s, there was no official diagnosis for depression in children according to the National Institute of Mental Health. Today that organization estimates that 2.5 million youngsters under eighteen have experienced clinical depression, so that its possibility cannot be dismissed offhand. Furthermore, once a young person has experienced a major depression, he or she is at risk of developing another depression within the next five years.

All children going through family troubles can be expected to experience a certain amount of moodiness and sadness, making true depression in its early stages difficult to identify. Although depression is often thought of as an adult problem, children can and do experience it in an equally serious way in times of conflict and stress.

Depression is a sad, energy-less state that can persist over periods of several months or more. Depression in children and teenagers manifests itself somewhat differently from depression in adults. Some ways that it can appear are as hyperactivity, fabricated illness, and aggression. Common symptoms are recognizable if the adults around are paying attention, a role that can fall to the grandparent in some situations.

The following symptoms can point to childhood depression when they are exhibited in multiple combinations:

severe changes in schoolwork
severe changes in eating or sleeping habits
withdrawal from friends and activities previously enjoyed
overreaction to criticism
changes in socialization
disturbance of sleeping and eating patterns
despair and hopelessness
ideas or threats of suicide
unhappy faces
complaints of illness when well
sexual promiscuity and delinquency in adolescents

Early diagnosis and treatment by a child and adolescent psychiatrist are essential for children with depression. The diagnosis could include psychological testing, laboratory testing, and consultation with other medical specialists. Mental health services are generally effective in treating childhood depression, but only if the adults in the child's life are aware of the condition and are willing to admit that it exists and needs attention. A grandparent who buys into the full meaning of this rule is in an excellent position to do so.

# THE DEVASTATION OF DIVORCE

Divorce is as devastating to grandparents as it is to parents and grandchildren. The knowledge that grandchildren are divorce casualties is a harsh reality to face. Whether the grandparents live nearby or far away, it is a time when their comfort and understanding can play a vital role in their grandchildren's well-being.

When two people marry and have children, they generally do so with the intention of living together happily for the rest of their lives. Today, given divorce statistics, the likelihood of such marital longevity is not great.

Over the last few years, an increasing amount of attention has been given to divorce by the Academy of Pediatrics. While it was generally thought children are resilient enough to handle divorce, it is now recognized that divorce has a lasting effect on as many as 30% of the children involved.

A common factor found among these children was the fact that hardly any of them had received help and close support from grandparents or other close relatives. It was felt that their later depression could have been avoided if counseling had been provided and if more time had been spent individually with them at the time of the divorce.

Divorce causes anxiety in children, and one common response is the release of angry behaviors and behaviors like noisy outbursts. Other expressions of anger can include bed-wetting, arguing, yelling, reverting to babyish behaviors, and refusing to talk about feelings. Unfortunately, behaviors like these can make already stressed parents recoil and distance themselves from their already fragile children.

> One of the most effective roles that grandparents can play in divorce (as long as grandchildren are not in any danger) is to stay out of the fray!

This will almost always be easier said than done for one of the divorcing parties is their own adult child. Nevertheless, if grandparents can focus on the good of their grandchildren, it is a commitment that can be successfully made and carried out. The tactful grandparent can let the adult child know that they understand their hurt and pain, but that they will be focusing their energies on helping the grandchildren come out as emotionally healthy as possible.

Many grandparents torture themselves with questions about why they didn't see it coming, or if they could have helped in some way to prevent the final split. Divorce can bring on doubts about the many things one did, or didn't do. The affected grandchildren are wondering the same things and feeling the same guilt and confusion.

Nobody has totally satisfactory answers and no grandparent can patch a broken marriage, or predict the final outcome as the lives are taken apart and painfully reassembled. Whenever possible, it is best to focus on being open and impartial with both parents and grandchildren—a huge undertaking! The ability to do so, along with the fact that a grandparent may be the only person involved who understands the benefits of doing so, could be critical to the grandchildren's ultimate adjustment. When viewed this way, is that really too much to ask?

Children need sufficient reinforcement that the divorce is not their fault, and reassurance that they will not be abandoned as a result of it. Talking to children about the separation or divorce in an open and honest way is the parents' job, but grandparents can be supportive by being there or by helping them with the answers ahead of time. In a recent guidance bulletin, the Academy of Pediatrics suggests having answers for at least the following questions:

> When the two adults that the grandchildren depend on the most are angry at each other, they need someone in their lives who is calm, loving, and nonjudgmental.

Why are you getting divorced?

Will you ever get back together again?

Where am I going to live?

Was the divorce my fault?

Will I have to change schools?

How often will I see Daddy/Mommy?

Will I still be able to see my friends?

Will I still be able to see my grandparents?

Are we going to be poor?

Can I still go to summer camp?

Who will I spend holidays with?

Distance is no obstacle to making the close kinds of personal contact that can bolster the sadness children are likely to feel during and after divorce. In fact, it is quite likely that a caring and concerned telephone call is one of the best medicines possible. Grandparents can relay messages that everyone in the family is experiencing a deep sense of sadness, and that it can be gotten through together.

Grandparents who are dealing with divorce can provide support by having their support and strategies firmly in place so that they are not swept up in explosive and emotional arguments and confrontations. The following are useful suggestions for strategies that can be used whenever challenges come up:

Advice will not be given to either parent.

Grandparents will be available for both sides to talk to.

Only positive things will be said about either parent
  to the children.
Grandparents are available if grandchildren need to get away.
Grandparents will be loving and attentive to the grandchildren
  whenever they need it.
Grandparents will not take sides.

This is a big order, considering the personal pain involved, but divorce is a time to rise above the ordinary. Everyone needs to be assured that the decision to follow these suggestions is grounded in a desire to safeguard the good of the grandchildren. It should be difficult for anyone to argue with such motivation.

Should children have access to both parents after a divorce? In developmental terms, the best parent is both parents. Unfortunately, nearly half of all children from divorced families have little or no contact with an absent parent. Unless there was an abusive situation, this is not a healthy situation for any child. The emotional loss of a loved one can affect them for the rest of their lives.

Children need to know that they can be with either parent when they feel the need to, regardless of the adult issues. There will be plenty of time later in their adult lives for them to make judgments about what has taken place. Even grandparents who really believe that one parent or the other was wrong, do their grandchildren no favor by sharing that opinion at this time.

Grandparents can help to provide neutral ground by arranging settings where time together with either parent can be turmoil free. They can also provide quality time instead of attempting to distract with gimmicks like presents and treats as grandchildren struggle to make sense of, and rebuild their broken world.

Divorce might seem like the ultimate disaster, but in the bigger picture the most damaging part (seeing parents fighting and out of control) is frequently over by the time the physical separation has taken place. The time after a divorce can be used by grandparents to focus on their grandchildren, and to model how to get on with the good parts of life. Grandparents can demonstrate that it is possible to let go of the negative things that have overshadowed the family.

Children, who once viewed their world as stable and unchanging are likely to experience a great deal of confusion as a result of unforeseen changes, and of the unpredictability of the days ahead. Grandparents are in a unique position to give the kinds of calm and encouraging advice that can help grandchildren feel more in control of their lives. If either parent is able to assist, so much the better. If not, grandparents can do this on their own.

No one, not even a grandparent, can eliminate the harsh realities of divorce, but grandparents can help grandchildren begin to look at some of the valuable, positive lessons that will emerge.

It is important to approach each grandchild as an individual when dealing with divorce. The focus on positive growth lessons will be more meaningful when directed to a particular grandchild. When a grandchild is willing to talk about any aspect of the divorce, that dialogue should be encouraged through talks and visits, or letters and phone calls. Grandchildren can be encouraged to express their feelings out loud, or in writing, respecting the trust and confidentiality that they place on the grandparent.

Grandparents are in excellent positions to touch their grandchildren's souls with their healing grandparent love. Exploring some of the following concepts with grandchildren can help to get them started on expressing the things that are upsetting to them.

- Life is always changing.
- A bad situation is never a permanent one.
- Each person chooses how changes will look.
- Trying out new ways to do things can be an adventure.
- Problems can be solved.
- Pain can be managed.
- People who love and care are the best resources.
- It is okay to feel anything without being ashamed.
- Everyone feels alone or lonely sometimes.

Age appropriate books can also help children to process and understand their feelings. Some good ones recommended by the Stepfamily Association of America include *Dinosaur's Divorce* by Laurence Krasny Brown and Marc Brown (ages 4 to 8) and *But . . . What About Me* by Bonnie Doss and Joyce Spindle (ages 5 to 18).

# LEGAL RIGHTS AND VISITATION

In some situations it doesn't matter how hard grandparents try, they can still be cut off from their grandchildren. This can happen in a number of situations, including bitter divorces, incarceration of a parent, the remarriage of a parent, or the placement of a grandchild in foster care.

If persistent efforts to make contact by phone and mail fail, a grandparent's last recourse might need to be legal action. Following this path can prove futile and expensive, but fortunately more and more states are passing laws to assure grandparent visitation. Such requests are easiest if presented at the time of legal proceedings as it can be difficult to come back to court for rights at a later date. Even if a grandparent is granted visitation, it can be revoked at a later date if there is a remarriage.

In many states, grandparent visitation is not automatic, which surprises many grandparents. A formal legal visitation request will have to prove that spending time with the grandparent will be in the child's best interest. The best interest usually includes consideration of the emotional ties that already exist, the nature of the current relationship, the grandparent's mental and physical health, the wishes of the grandchildren (if they are old enough to express them), and the grandparent's willingness to cooperate with other family members. (One more good reason to remain as impartial as possible!)

Going to court should be the last resort, used only after trying to reach an agreement with whoever has custody. That is less expensive and less stressful, as well as friendlier, making it better for the grandchildren involved.

Private mediation is another route. A mediator is an expert in assisting people to resolve disagreements. Mediation is always voluntary, so the custodial person has to be willing to try and neither side can be forced to agree to anything. Some private attorneys and other professionals will offer their services as mediators.

An advantage to filing a court petition if the avenues mentioned fail is that courts require the parties to participate in court mediation services. In many cases, an expensive legal battle can be avoided at this point in the process.

# GRANDPARENT CUSTODY

At the last census (1990) some 3.2 million children were found to be living with grandparents or other relatives. These numbers are continually climbing. Grandparent custody cuts across ethnic, social, and economic lines, catching many of the affected grandparents completely off guard.

Grandparents have long assumed a role in caring for grandchildren in the event of death, but today they are doing so as the result of teenage pregnancy, substance abuse, divorce, incarceration, neglect, abandonment, AIDS, physical and mental illness, and other debilitating social problems. Instead of being able to enjoy

> How many grandparents sit by their windows watching neighborhood children playing while wishing that they could have another family? How many would start all over again if they had a chance?

their golden years, they find themselves overwhelmed with financial, emotional, and legal concerns associated with custody.

Many grandchildren in grandparent custody require special educational and psychological and medical interventions to help get them back onto a normal track. A great many have been at risk of being (or have been) physically or mentally abused in their short lives. When you consider the importance of a stable childhood experience in producing a happy and successful adult, the enormous challenges that grandparent custody carries with it should be obvious.

Taking on the parenting role in middle or old age generally means the end of life as it has been, and the beginning of one not willingly chosen. Feelings of fear, anger, and depression are as common as the tasks of grappling with paperwork, legal, medical, and emotional issues. Yet, despite the enormous burden that custody entails, there is generally some peace gained from the grandparent's decision to take action.

Once the decision is made, there is a resolve to move forward toward healing. As positive actions are taken, past tragedies can be left behind. In spite of the seemingly unlimited new responsibilities, more and more resources are becoming available to assist custodial grandparents so that it is no longer necessary to do everything alone.

# GRANDCHILDREN WHO GET INTO TROUBLE

It isn't an easy world to grow up in and not every grandchild emerges unscathed from negative influences. Not every grandchild turns out to be charming, articulate, motivated, and successful. What can grandparents make of grandchildren who seem to be headed in the wrong direction? And how should they treat them and their parents?

These are difficult questions and the answers depend largely on the age of the rebellious grandchild and the ways in which the defiance is being acted out. Angry school-age children may not actually get into trouble, but they can cause a great deal of family turbulence with their antisocial and belligerent attitudes. They might be passing through a stage and grandparents can try to keep the lines of communication open so that someone in the family knows what is going on. A grandparent might be viewed by teenage grandchildren as the only adult who is not picking on them.

Rebellion in teenagers is common and usually passes, although it can seem extreme at the time. If the child is not in legal trouble and the grandparent is willing, they might consider the role of sounding board for the troubled youngster. Sometimes, teenage rebellion just has to be waited out with the grandchild knowing that the people they love have faith that they will make it through. At other times, it will require a concerted and decisive action.

Grandparents can always make the constancy of their love known without condoning undesirable behaviors. A grandparent has known a grandchild for many years and has a history to draw on when helping them to view and reconcile life issues.

> Grandparents can remind their grandchildren of the good qualities they have seen over the years. They can help grandchildren to recall the times that have been enjoyed together.

## EXPLORING RULE 12 CONCEPTS

*The following issues can help you to be aware of difficulties that some grandparents must work through:*

### 1. Do I know that things can go wrong despite my best efforts?

*Always:*
• But continue to focus on the positive.

*Sometimes:*
• But make sure you work to give your best.

- Accept that even if you don't always give your best, you are still not responsible for what goes wrong.
- Don't automatically avoid the uncomfortable.

*Never:*
- You are in denial.

## 2. Do I know my physical and mental limits and work to uphold them?

*Always:*
- And you resist the need to feel guilty or selfish for this.

*Sometimes:*
- Write down your most important limits so they are clear in your mind (will not be yelled at, made to feel guilty, agree to give unreasonably).
- Picture the parents when they put you in a defensive position. How do they accomplish this? How can you break that pattern?
- Practice saying, "I need to do this for me."

*Never:*
- You are apparently at their beck and call.

## 3. Do I remain neutral in family arguments?

*Always:*
- This is an honest approach to watching out for grandchildren.

*Sometimes:*
- Try walking out of the room and reading grandchildren a book instead of being drawn in.
- Practice this skill so that it becomes natural and takes no thought.
- Acknowledge to yourself that both parents are human and forgive as much as is possible.

*Never:*
- You are robbing your grandchildren of the impartial insider that they may need some day.

## 4. Do I respect my children's spouses?

*Always:*
- It is the person your child has chosen to spend life with.

*Sometimes:*
- Remember that slipups can tend to stick around.

  Words spoken cannot be taken back.

- Feeling something doesn't mean that you have to act out on it.

*Never:*

- You could star in the movie *The In-law from Hell!*

## 5. Do I respect their confidence when grandchildren talk to me?

*Always:*

- You understand the importance of nurturing trust in your relationships with them.
- Unless it is something serious that the parents need to know.

*Sometimes:*

- This is hard, but the reward is a peek into a child's soul.
- Grandchildren can be embarrassed if you repeat things that they meant only for you.

*Never:*

- They have long since stopped telling you anything!

## 6. Can I turn down grandchildren's requests when they are unreasonable or unwise?

*Always:*

- But you try to help them understand why and you assure them of your confidentiality.

*Sometimes:*

- It can be shortsighted to only focus getting them out of an immediate fix.
- Older grandchildren have been known to take advantage of good nature and their grandparent's love for them.
- Resist falling into the trap of becoming emotional over every problem that they confide in you.

*Never:*

- Such behavior can only worsen the situation.

FINAL
THOUGHTS

## GIVING AND GETTING THE BEST

At this point you have probably begun to experiment with ways to alter your grandparent outlook. Perhaps you are beginning to see positive results from your more carefully targeted efforts. Armed with the sense of understanding about which rules you are choosing to break, and actually beginning to do so, can allow you to achieve unparalleled success and satisfaction as a grandparent.

This is all part of a purposeful shifting away from what is *expected* of you toward what is *needed* from you. If your actions remain focused on outcomes that are centered on your grandchildren, you are bound to feel more comfortable and certain that you are on the right track.

Breaking the rules can give your grandchildren the sense of continuity that is difficult to attain in today's hectic world. The need has never been greater for grandparents who are willing to give grandchildren a greater sense of belonging in their family group. It is not unusual for grandchildren to spend most all of their waking hours with peers at school, at child care, and in a community activity or other team sports programs. It is less and less common to find them engaged in meaningful interactions with caring adults, so that the time you spend with them is more critical than ever.

What children need most from their grandparents today is high-quality, purposeful attention; attention that makes them know that they are loved, cherished, and valued.

This cannot be accomplished by stuffing grandchildren's mouths with cookies and their hands with gifts. Nor can it happen when grandparents overwhelm already stressed families with biased advice and self-centered opinions. The family structure has become one delicate balancing act and it is badly in need of family members, like grandparents, who can reinforce its structural soundness and help to shore it up, when that is necessary.

Breaking the rules creates strong grandparents who know how to focus on their grandchildren, and who are buddies and confidants to them as well. It also creates grandparents who are not willing to be martyrs or scapegoats and who are willing to set limits and instigate guidelines that protect their own personal space and integrity—exactly as grandchildren must learn to do!

The payoffs far exceed the investment of time and thought you are willing to put into it. By continuing to question your attitudes, motivations, and actions, you can all but guarantee marvelous grandparenting days now, tomorrow, and well into your future!

APPENDIX

# GRANDPARENT RESOURCES

## BOOKS FOR PARENTS/GRANDPARENTS

### Child Care and Development

Dorothy Einon, *Learning Early: Everything Parent's Need to Encourage and Develop Their Child's Learning Skills from Birth to Six Years of Age*. New York: Facts On File, 1999.

Jane M. Healy, *Your Child's Growing Mind: A Guide to Learning and Brain Development from Birth to Adolescence*. New York: Main Street Books, 1994.

Steven P. Shevlov et al. eds., *Caring for Your Baby and Young Child: Birth to Age 5*. New York: Bantam Doubleday Dell, 1998.

Edward Schor, ed., *Caring for Your School-Age Child: Ages 5 to 12*. New York: Bantam Doubleday Dell, 1996.

### Communication

John Christie, *What If . . .? 450 Thought-Provoking Questions to Get Your Kids Talking, Laughing, and Thinking*. Grand Rapids, Mich.: Zondervan Pub., 1996.

Frances Presma and Paula Edelson, *Straight Talk About Today's Families*. New York: Facts On File, 1999.

## Depression

David Fassler and Lynne Dumas, *"Help Me, I'm Sad": Recognizing, Treating, and Preventing Childhood and Adolescent Depression.* New York: Penguin, 1998.

Cytryn, McKnew, and Wiener, *Growing Up Sad.* New York: W. W. Norton, 1998.

## Discipline

Edward Christophersen, *Beyond Discipline.* New York: Overland Press, 1997.

Henry Cloud and John Townsend, *Boundaries with Kids: When to Say Yes, When to Say No to Help Your Children Gain Control of Their Lives.* Grand Rapids, Mich.: Zondervan, 1998.

## Divorce

Vicki Lansky, *Divorce Book for Parents.* Minnetonka, Minn.: Book Peddlers, 1996.

Debbie Barr, *Children of Divorce.* Grand Rapids, Mich.: Zondervan Pub., 1992.

Kay Marie Porterfield, *Straight Talk About Divorce.* New York: Facts On File, 1999.

## Health

*American Medical Association Complete Guide to Your Children's Health.* New York: Random House, 1999.

William Feldman, M.D., *The 3 A.M. Handbook: The Most Commonly Asked Questions About Your Child's Health.* New York: Facts On File, 1998.

Miriam Stoppard, M.D., *Complete Baby and Child Care.* New York: DK Publishing, 1995.

## Nutrition

Joy Bauer, *The Complete Idiot's Guide to Eating Smart.* Malibu, Calif.: Alpha Books, 1997.

## Toilet Training

Joanna Cole, *Parents Book of Toilet Training.* New York: Ballantine Books, 1990.

Alison Mack, *Toilet Learning: The Picture Book Technique for Children and Parents.* Boston: Little Brown & Co., 1983.

# BOOKS FOR KIDS

## Cooking

Marianne Mayer, *The Mother Goose Cookbook: Rhymes and Recipes for the Very Young*. New York: William Morrow and Co., 1998.

Barbara Walker, *The Little House Cookbook: Frontier Foods from Laura Ingalls Wilder's Classic Stories*. New York: Harper Trophy, 1995.

Roald Dahl, *Roald Dahl's Revolting Recipes*. New York: Viking Children's Books, 1994.

## Divorce

Laurence Krasny Brown and Marc Tolon Brown, *Dinosaurs Divorce: A Guide for Changing Families*. Reprint. Boston: Little, Brown, 1988.

Bonnie Doss and Joyce Spindle, *But . . . What About Me*. Corpus Christi, Texas: Bookmark Publishing, 1998.

Richard Gardner, *The Boys and Girls Book About Divorce*. New York: Bantam Young Readers reissue, 1985.

## Money

Sam Berenstain, *The Berenstain Bears' Trouble with Money Book*. New York: Random House, 1998.

Lynette Long, *One Dollar: My First Book About Money*. Hauppauge, N.Y.: Barron's Juveniles, 1998.

Steven Otfinoski, *The Kid's Guide to Money: Earning It, Saving It, Spending It, Growing It, Sharing It*. New York: Scholastic, 1996.

## Toilet Training

Fred Rogers, *Going to the Potty*. New York: PaperStar, 1997.

# GRANDPARENT SUPPORT ORGANIZATIONS

AARP Grandparent Information Center
American Association of Retired Persons
601 E Street, NW. Washington, DC 20049
(202) 434-2296 or 2108.

Caring Grandparents of America
400 7th Street NW
Suite 302
Washington, DC 20024-2206

Grandparents Raising Grandchildren
P.O. Box 104
Colleyville, TX 76034
(817) 577-0435

National Coalition of Grandparents
137 Larkin Street
Madison, WI 53705
(601) 238-8751

R.O.C.K.I.N.G. (Raising Our Children's Kids: An Intergenerational
    Network of Grandparenting, Inc.)
P.O. Box 96
Niles, MI 49120
(616) 683-9038.

# WHAT GRANDPARENTS LOVE AND FEAR

When asked to comment on their views of their relationships with their grandchildren, the following comments were elicited from selected grandparents in Hemet, California:

" I wish these children could have a safer world to grow up in; less violence and less pollution. We love watching them develop from year to year. They give us so much pleasure. "

" There is so much violence on television and videos. Children really need more emphasis on morals and spiritual guidance. Working parents need to learn to spend at least some quality time with their children every day. "

" Grandparenting is an important function in life. It can give a child an opportunity to become involved with a different generation and to learn about their experiences with life. "

" We love to entertain them, knowing that we can send them home afterward. The smallest one whines because she can't do what her brothers do, but that is normal. And, oh! The behavior of the teenagers! "

" We enjoyed playing with them when they were younger. We attended their sports and church activities. As they grow older, we are interested in their educational goals. They help us keep up with the current fashions and lifestyle trends. We wish they lived closer. "

" We love it when they come to visit and spend the night. Anything goes at Grandma and Grandpa's. We stock up the refrigerator with special treats and sometimes the happy noise is overwhelming! We are happy to see them leave and suddenly the house is too quiet again. "

" I never hear from my grandchildren unless I make the effort. I send gifts and never even know if they are received. "

" They are never shy with hugs and kisses. We love them to spend the night. For breakfast we use the fine china and crystal glasses. They deserve the best! "

" We love them all the same, but we do have the younger ones over more often, as they live closer. The fourteen-year-old says that when the going gets tough at home, he goes to Grandma's. "

" My seventeen-year-old grandson has a poor relationship with his father because he was on drugs and went to prison. I have a good relationship with him. He shows artistic attributes, which we enjoy. "

" I worry that so many children have to come home alone after school. They don't mind as well without supervision. There is more crime. Parents may earn more, but they aren't giving their children more in the long run. "

" My grandson is too trusting and unaware of people. I try not to criticize him and to be there for him, but I don't like his ponytail. He is so good looking and I will be glad when he is through his hair ordeal. "

# WHAT TEENAGERS REMEMBER ABOUT THEIR GRANDPARENTS

When they have grown up and become young adults, teenagers have formed definite concepts of how their grandparents affected them during their early years. The following sample of comments come from high school students in the suburb of Carmichael, California:

" I didn't get to see my grandmother very much, but when I did, I loved it! I looked up to her and she definitely affected me with her love. She was loving, funny, strong, and everything that I want to be. She died in 1988, but I will always love her. " (Age 15.)

" My grandmother shows me that you can actually grow younger as you age. She is a terrific role model who never ceases to amaze me! " (Age 16.)

" My grandmother always caused problems in our house between my mom and dad. I hated her for that. She helped me see how I never want to treat people. " (Age 16.)

" She was the lady I spent my summers with while my parents worked. Sometimes I thought she was being mean, but now I know she cared deep down. My grandfather would always hide and jump out and try to scare me. He gave me my peculiar, twisted sense of humor. " (Age 17.)

" Visiting my grandmother was always so special. I cherish it to this day. When it was time to go home, she always gave us little bags for the ride home. There were special treats and things in the bags that we loved. She always cared enough to prepare for our time together so that it would be special. " (Age 18.)

" My grandfather taught me how to whittle, how to make a tire swing, and how to ski and fish. He even let me drive his tractor, which made me feel important. My grandmother let me pick strawberries in the garden and taught me to shuck corn. Most important, they taught me that even if you are far away from someone, you can still be close at heart. " (Age 18.)

# CONGRESSIONAL "YEAR OF THE GRANDPARENT" PROCLAMATION

In 1994, Congress issued a joint resolution noting the important role that grandparents play in the family fiber of this nation. That proclamation reads as follows:

U.S. Congress, House Joint Resolution No. 355
103rd Congress, 2D Session, April 19, 1994

## JOINT RESOLUTION
*Designating 1995 as the "Year of the Grandparent"*

Whereas grandparents bring a tremendous amount of love and power for good into the lives of their grandchildren;

Whereas grandparents, in partnership with parents, help deepen every child's roots and strengthen every child's wings so that every child may soar into adulthood with a glad heart and a confident spirit;

Whereas grandparents are a strong and important voice in support of the happiness and well-being of children;

Whereas many aspects of being a grandparent are incredibly rewarding and just plain fun;

Whereas grandparents should be acknowledged for the important role they play within families, and for the many and varied contributions they make to enhance and further the value of the family and family traditions;

Whereas public awareness of and appreciation for the contributions of grandparents should be strengthened;

Whereas grandparents should be encouraged to continue as a vital force in the shaping of American families today and into the future;

Whereas the Nation currently acknowledges the contributions of grandparents celebrating National Grandparents Day each September; and

Whereas there should be a year-long celebration of grandparents and grandparenting;

Now, therefore, be it resolved by the Senate and the House of Representatives of the United States of America in Congress assembled, that 1995 is designated as the "Year of the Grandparent," and the President is authorized and requested to issue a proclamation calling on the people of the United States to observe the year with appropriate programs, ceremonies, and activities.

# INDEX